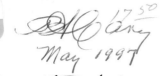

1692
WITCH HUNT

The Layman's Guide
to the
Salem Witchcraft Trials

By

George Malcolm Yool

HERITAGE
BOOKS,
INC.

Published 1992 By

HERITAGE BOOKS, INC.
1540E Pointer Ridge Place, Bowie, Maryland 20716
(301) 390-7709

ISBN 1-55613-565-3

A Complete Catalog Listing Hundreds of Titles on
History, Genealogy and Americana
Free on Request

To the victims of 1692, Massachusetts,
who sacrificed so much for what they believed,
and their descendants,
this book is dedicated.

PREFACE

This book is based on several accurate accounts of the Salem witchcraft hysteria that occurred between the years 1692 and 1693. The historical facts, as chilling as they may be, are true. Exact dates have been included where available. Most depositions, written courtroom testimony, and miscellaneous documents have been paraphrased from the originals into Twentieth Century English for easy reading. Punctuation, mostly in the form of commas, was added to separate the long unpunctuated sentences. Some terms were left unchanged since they do not have a direct translation. For example, the word Goody was substituted for the first name of both men and women when their first name was unknown, or out of respect. Careful reading of the surrounding text should make clear an archaic word's meaning.

Over 200 people were imprisoned for witchcraft; about the same number fled. If a person didn't come to trial, in most cases, there would be no further record of that person. The reader can assume that he or she spent several months in prison, heavily shackled and chained, after which, he or she was given full amnesty. If I found a later, non-trial related record of that person, it immediately follows the hearing for said person. Some of the people who fled before their arrest could be completed had interesting stories to tell. These stories have been included for the reader's enjoyment.

There are a few important points I had to follow to make this book more enjoyable. In most cases I followed exact chronology. However, when more than one situation arose at the same instant in time, I took the liberty of completing one person's story before beginning the other. The modern Gregorian calendar didn't come into use until 1752. The calendar in use by England during this earlier period was the Julian calendar. March 25 was the first day of the new year. So as not to confuse the reader, dates have been adjusted to modern convention. This holds true even for verbatim transcripts.

Because of the multitude of similar names, I followed those names with Junior or Senior. To refresh the reader's memory, relationships between key individuals are repeated at intervals, and the person's previous history is outlined before his or her trial. Throughout the book the reader will see the term "afflicted children". I used this term rather than be redundant with a long list of names. Most of them appeared at each hearing or trial. Twelve-year old Ann Putnam Junior seems to have been the main and deadliest witness at all prosecutions. Her full, public confession is at the end of this book. Below is a list of all the "afflicted children", for the reader's reference:

Sarah Bibber (36) - no other information available.
Elizabeth Booth (18) - no other information available.
Sarah Churchill (20) - servant of George Jacobs Senior.
Elizabeth Hubbard (17) - niece of Doctor John Griggs.
Mercy Lewis (19) - servant of Thomas Putnam.
Elizabeth Parris (9) - daughter of Reverend Samuel Parris.
Gertrude Pope (older woman) - suffered from temporary insanity.
Ann Putnam Junior (12) - daughter of Thomas Putnam.
Ann Putnam Senior (30) - wife of Thomas Putnam.
Susanna Sheldon (18) - no other information available.
Mary Walcott (17) - daughter of Captain Jonathan Walcott.
Mary Warren (20) - servant of John Proctor.
Abigail Williams (11) - niece of Reverend Samuel Parris.

Keep in mind as you read this book that the Puritan people of Salem Village (now known as Danvers) were in a state of economic upheaval, torn between being a suburb of Salem Town and the desire to become an independent city. For the first crucial months, the court system was in turmoil, having lost its charter in 1689. Because of this, no trials could be held. If a speedy trial had been possible, some of the events might have been different. Instead the system became backlogged and had to be rushed, at the expense of the persons involved.

The terrible things that occurred in this short period should serve as a warning to people everywhere. This book shows how easy it is to come to the wrong conclusions when the whole truth of a matter is neither sought nor wanted.

Our judicial system, though not perfect, has come a long way since this tragedy, and one can't help but feel that this black time in American history played a significant role in its development.

I must thank both the Essex Institute of Salem, Massachusetts, whose invaluable assistance set me on the right historical path, and the County of Essex, Commonwealth of Massachusetts, for their kind and generous help in providing the material I sorely needed to complete this book.

For those readers that would like to study some of the original documents, there is a three-volume set entitled *The Salem Witchcraft Papers*; these are verbatim transcripts of the legal documents of the Salem witchcraft outbreak of 1692, by Paul Boyer and Stephen Nissenbaum, editors; DaCapo Press, New York, 1977. Although it is out of print, most university libraries have a copy. If your local library doesn't have it, they can borrow it through the lending library service.

The Author

INTRODUCTION

The Time: Winter, 1691
The Place: Salem Village (Danvers), Massachusetts

Huddled around a roaring fire, a small group of young girls listened intently as the West Indian slave, Tituba, wove her tales of spells and black magic. These stories were unlike anything the children had ever heard before in their restricted community, where acting did not exist and education was at its lowest ebb. This harmless scene evolved into one of the darkest periods in American history, the Salem witchcraft trials.

For most of 1692, this handful of bored children held the lives of hundreds of people in their hands. Sadly, several innocent people would lose their lives and property before hysteria was replaced by reason.

What really happened? How did the public become so deeply involved? What were the true circumstances surrounding the trials? What myths had their roots in this period, and who was really to blame? These are only some of the questions answered in the book, *1692 Witch Hunt: The Layman's Guide to the Salem Witchcraft Trials.*

A chronological account of the event from its humble beginning in 1691 to its dramatic conclusion in 1957, the book contains a wealth of information gleaned from museums, court records and the personal archives of the descendants on both sides of the conflict. Most of the material contained in the book hasn't been available to the general public for several years. The author has transcribed several documents into contemporary English so that the modern reader can feel the true impact of their content. Except for punctuation, others, like Bridget Bishop's death warrant, were left in their original Old English form.

Several prominent people wrote books and kept diaries during the trials. For the reader's enjoyment, their first-hand observations are included, along with a short history of each person. The last chapter contains the confessions and written public apologies of some of the main participants in this tragedy, along with their post-trial histories.

What happened in Massachusetts holds a fascination for people all over the world. With more than two years of intensive research behind it, this book should prove to contain a wealth of information for anyone interested in the roots of this American tragedy. For the casual reader, the true story, more chilling than any work of fiction, will keep him on the edge of his seat.

CHAPTER I

THE PEOPLE OF 1692

A Brief Insight

Before I delve into the events of 1692, I need to put everything into perspective for the Twentieth-Century reader.

I must strongly caution the reader to avoid imposing his moral standards on the people of 1692. They were very moral and outgoing. The Puritan faith was a very personable one. Their belief in the freedom of religion was one of the reasons they came to America. The persecution they had experienced from the Inquisition was still freshly emblazoned on their minds. Puritans lived in harmony with several other faiths. The first one that comes to mind was the Quakers. What happened in 1692 wasn't a Puritan thing, as some books would like you to believe. It was an hysterical reaction to some incidents of minor significance by the people in New England.

The trials were caused by several factors, the majority of which had nothing to do with religion. Instead, most of the accusations stemmed from revenge, jealousy and greed - human frailties that everyone has, to some extent, no matter how pious they are.

The people of New England had lived in close harmony for years; in fact, too close. Everyone knew everybody else's business. If a man was seeing somebody else's wife, the whole town knew about it. Death at an early age was commonplace. Physicians were still in the Dark Ages, their medicines consisting mainly of home-made concoctions that seemed to work on some diseases. If the doctor couldn't relieve the patient after several tries, he usually blamed it on an unknown spirit. This diagnosis wasn't questioned by the people, they **all** believed in such things. New England was in the midst of the French and Indian War. A drought had stricken the area and their government was in turmoil. The court system

1

was nonexistent; they had no charter. These things had produced uncertainty in the people's minds.

The events started in Salem Village, a small farming community 15 miles north of Boston. For several years arguments had been raging between the village inhabitants and the people in Topsfield over land boundaries and ownership.

The town of Salem wanted Salem Village to become part of them; the village wanted to break away and become a separate town. Rich people were coming in and buying up land. The people of the village were poor farmers and resented the influx of new people telling them what to do. Several court battles ensued between the villagers and the rich outsiders. The outsiders won most of the disputes. Bitterness developed and festered for several years. Some of the testimony at the trials reflects this.

In the early months of 1692, a little nine-year-old girl named Elizabeth Parris (possibly for attention from her very busy and troubled father, Samuel Parris) started the whole thing. If she had been the only one to have fits, nothing would have developed. At the time, Elizabeth's cousin was living with her, and, seeing the attention everyone gave that little girl, Elizabeth felt she should have some as well. It wasn't very long before most of the young girls in the neighborhood joined suit.

Even then nothing should have come of it. However, the parents were at their wits end, and a doctor was called. He knew that these fits were beyond his skills to cure, so he announced that the children were possessed by demons.

Samuel Parris was the minister of Salem Village. He had been in an ongoing battle with the village for some time. At the time the incident with his daughter occurred, he was under great stress. He knew that the village was about to terminate him.

Rev. Parris and his friend, Edward Putnam, kept asking the girls who afflicted them. At first they kept silent, but the constant cross examination finally broke them down. They named three people who were considered low-lifes by the children's parents. One woman was a slave, who liked to dabble in voodoo and fortune telling. She had kept the girls occupied during the winter months by teaching them about these things. The second woman was very poor and foulmouthed. She and her children were constantly without a place to stay. The third was a woman who had a rather flamboyant lifestyle; the local women disliked her entertaining their husbands to all hours of the night. Samuel Parris and Edward Putnam pressed charges against them.

When these three women were brought in for their hearing, it

2

should have been the end of it, but the slave woman did an unexpected thing. She confessed to being a witch. By confessing, she started a chain of events that would create an avalanche of accusations. People that had animosities toward the other two women came forward and accused them of anything that would make them appear to be guilty. The afflicted young girls liked the limelight and started adding names of others that afflicted them. The names added to the list were drawn from people the girls or their parents had been at odds with. Some of the villagers came down with similar symptoms of affliction and accused people they had grudges against.

Accusations spread to other villages, then to the town of Salem itself. The town of Andover became devastated, but more about this in other chapters.

Somewhere in all of this, Samuel Parris saw a way of becoming so popular that the village would want him to stay on as minister. He likened it to a religious battle between him and Satan. Thomas Putnam's family saw it as a way to get revenge on some of the people that had done things to them in the past, especially those that had caused the deaths of several of their friends and neighbors.

As the accusations increased, people became fearful for the lives of their loved ones. When a member of the family was accused, the other family members would try to talk that member into confessing that he or she was a witch. This was done because of a strange quirk in the law. The law stated that anyone that confessed was to be forgiven and all those that didn't were to be executed. Because of this, more and more people confessed. The judges felt, at least in the beginning, that their rigorous prosecutions were justified. If the trials were wrong, no one should have confessed.

The trials were mainly based on spectral evidence. The general belief was that the devil could only appear as the specter of a guilty person. Since the spectral evidence was seen only by those that were afflicted, no one could verify what the afflicted girls saw. The court accepted whatever the girls told them as the truth. By the time the ministers of Salem were able to correct this misconception, the trials had gone too far. It's quite possible that the judges were sorely embarrassed by their mistake, an understandable and very human reaction. They were supposed to be better informed and more capable than the average person, and most of them were newly elected to the first court under the new charter. When the people came to their senses, the same judges worked together toward the establishment of a better court system.

Before I talk about some of the ministers involved in this, I would like to point out that the existence of witches was never in question. Everyone believed in their existence, even the Indians.

Several ministers were involved in the trials; the most noteworthy were the Reverend Increase Mather and his son Cotton Mather.

Increase Mather, president of Harvard University, was the most powerful man in New England. His influence stretched all the way across the Atlantic to Mother England. He did more to shape New England than any other man of that period. Despite all this, he, like everyone else, believed in witches. But these trials bothered him and some of the other ministers. The spectral evidence wasn't acceptable proof. He and several ministers wrote an opinion to the court, at the court's request. That opinion was all but ignored by the court; it had come too late. Later, an expanded version in the form of a book was circulated and this helped to bring the terrible tragedy to a close.

Cotton Mather, unlike his father, was overzealous about the witch trials. He wanted to see the "old time religion" revived in the hearts of his constituents. He totally believed in spectral evidence. A very learned man with several good books to his credit, he was, aside from this one fault, a man to be respected.

The Reverend John Hale of Beverly was another minister who believed in the trials. He suspected something was wrong with the trials fairly early, some believe as early as August. When his wife was accused, he became certain and came to his senses. A very scholarly man, in 1702 he published *A Modest Enquiry Into the Nature of Witchcraft*. His account of the witchcraft episode is honest, balanced and unbiased. It is a worthy addition to anyone's library.

The Reverend Nicholas Noyes, was one of the prosecutors during the trials. He had the dubious task of extracting confessions from the accused. Like Samuel Parris, he pursued witchcraft with all his zeal. I can't say anything for him and will not say anything against him.

There are several people of note who were involved in the witch trials. I will touch briefly upon the lives of some of them.

Sir William Phips, Governor of Massachusetts, was a soldier of the highest caliber. When he returned from England with the new charter, he took on the position of governor. Because of the French and Indian War, he was forced to leave Massachusetts in the hands of his lieutenant governor, William Stoughton. Governor Phips went off to fight. While he was away the witch trials ran

4

rampant. Upon his return, he instigated reforms that brought the episode to an end.

Samuel Sewall was one of the judges at the trials. He was a fine statesman, judge, linguist and scholar. Like everyone else, he firmly believed in the trials, until one of his college friends was hanged. Samuel Sewall has the distinction of being the only judge that publicly apologized for his part in the witch trials. He was later elected Counselor and was reelected 33 times without interruption. He eventually became Chief Justice of the Superior Court. Samuel Sewall kept a diary for 56 years. It is a gold mine for the historian studying early New England life.

George Corwin, Sheriff, 26-years old, had the tough responsibility of arresting the people and collecting what was due the government. He appears to have been a little overzealous in his duties. Two of the judges were his uncles and one was his father-in-law. He might have done the things that he did to show his relatives they'd chosen the right man for the job, or he may have done them for capital gain. History hides the answers to such things under a blanket of eternal darkness.

The people of the period were, in this author's opinion, exceptionally good people. Their stories contain acts of bravery, courage, piety and heroism that stir the heart and bring tears to the eyes. Even the jury's public apology was given with a sincerity and humility seldom seen in the annuals of history.

As I said in the beginning of this short chapter, do not judge these people by your moral standards; judge them by their strengths.

CHAPTER II

IMPURE THOUGHTS

Winter, 1691 - March 21, 1692

Nine-year old Elizabeth Parris was a precocious child. Her father, the minister of Salem Village, ran a strict Puritanical household, giving her very little in the way of much needed attention. His ongoing feud with the town's elders had put him under a lot of pressure.

When he had been approached to take the job as town minister, the elders had indicated that he would be given possession of the parish house and its adjoining pasture. The contract he'd received stated that they were to remain in his care only while he was minister. Several arguments ensued between him and the townspeople over this matter, and by December 1691, he feared for his job.

Elizabeth had become friendly with one of her father's slaves, a woman from the West Indies named Tituba. Tituba and her husband, John Indian, had been raised in an atmosphere filled with superstitions, spells and potions. In the winter of 1691, Tituba's stories and knowledge of the black arts drew Elizabeth and several other girls to her warm fireside. They listened with great interest to her tales. She taught them how to mix potions and cast spells. The girls learned well. Soon they were showing off their palm-reading and fortune-telling skills. It was harmless, a friendly gathering that in normal circumstances wouldn't have caused any problems. But this period in Massachusetts was filled with zealousness and suspicion. American history was about to take a dark, unforgettable, path.

On January 20, 1692, Elizabeth took ill. She had just sat down to supper when her body became contorted. She fell on the floor and crawled under her chair. Twisting in a tormented fashion, she uttered some strange sounds like one possessed. This

7

behavior became more pronounced as the days went on.

Eleven-year old Abigail Williams was the niece of Mister Parris. Living in his household, she saw the extra attention that Elizabeth's antics were gleaning, and not wanting to be left out, she joined in on the fun. A few days later the other girls followed suit. Things were getting out of hand, so in mid-February Doctor William Griggs was called in to examine the girls.

Medical doctors were still in the dark ages in the Seventeenth Century. He examined them all very carefully, but their affliction was beyond his power to control. He, like many other doctors of his time, took the easy way out.

"They have been bewitched!" he said authoritatively.

No one questioned his diagnosis. Everyone knew that witches existed to do the biding of the Prince of Darkness.

As time went on, people from all over the countryside came to watch the girls. The townspeople took such fervent interest in them that they forgot their chores. It was a pitiful sight to behold and everyone made sure to see it. The sudden interest and notoriety was pleasing to the girls, so they intensified their antics. They took their fits into the streets. One Sunday they even had one in church. From then on, hardly a Sunday went by without at least one outburst. No one noticed that the fits never occurred in the middle of prayer, only during a lull in the service. This kept the people from getting annoyed with them.

Mister Parris, fearing for his daughter, asked other members of the clergy to come and study the girls. Maybe they would be able to come up with a solution to this perplexing situation.

The girls put on a show that astonished the ministers. They concluded that Doctor Griggs' diagnosis was absolutely correct. Nowhere in the world had they heard of such a blatant case of Satanic possession. These findings went around the town like wildfire. Angered, the townspeople became an unthinking mob. No one dared say anything or offer any evidence that this was not the work of the Devil.

The question everyone wanted answered was, "Who or what was causing these girls to act the way they were?"

It had to be a witch. Only a witch could control an innocent person. The question was put to the girls several times. Finally on February 29, the girls broke their silence. Three names were mentioned again and again: Sarah Good, Sarah Osborne and Tituba. Arrest warrants were issued.

On March 1, a preliminary hearing was conducted by the Right Honorable John Hathorne, ancestor to author Nathaniel Hawthorne and to Jonathan Corwin. The three suspects were led into the meetinghouse and stood up on a platform so all could see. After a prayer was said, two of the accused were led out of the room. The magistrates had taken note of the hostility toward Sarah Good and had decided to question her first. Sarah Good, was considered a woman of poor character who had a nagging attitude. She was dirt poor and her children had slept on the ground many times for lack of a home. She would have to go begging from door to door. She had no friends and a bad reputation. Pregnant and forsaken by her husband, the townspeople had no liking of her kind. It would be easy to find her guilty. The magistrates had made a wise choice.

"Sara Good, who is your familiar?"

"I don't have one."

"Have you made a contract with the Devil?"

"No."

"Why are you hurting these children?"

She looked at the children writhing in pain. "I'm not hurting them. It's terrible," she said.

"Who are you making do it?"

"No one."

"Then what creature are you making do it?"

"There is no creature. I'm innocent!" she said, rudely.

"Why did you leave Mister Parris's house, muttering?"

"I wasn't muttering. I was thanking him for something he gave one of my children!" she said.

"Have you made a contract with the Devil?"

"No, I haven't!!" she shouted.

Hathorne had the afflicted children come up to Mrs. Good. He then asked them if this was one of the people that was torturing them. They replied, "Yes," and started having fits again.

"Sarah Good, look what you have done. Why are you lying to us? Why are you torturing these children?"

"I'm not torturing them!!!"

"Who are you getting to do it?"

"No one. I detest it."

"How come they're being tormented?"

"How would I know? You brought other people here, but you're charging me with it."

"Why, who was it?"

"I don't know, but it must have been someone else you brought with you."

"We brought you here."

"But you brought in two others."

"Then who was it that tormented the children?"

"If anybody did it, it must have been Osborne," she said in desperation.

"What do you mutter when you walk away from people's houses?"

"If I have to tell you, I will."

"Do tell us then."

"If I have to tell you, I will. It's the Commandments. I hope I can say the Commandments."

"Which Commandment?"

"If I have to tell you, I will. It's a psalm."

"What psalm."

After a long time she muttered part of a psalm.

"Who do you serve?"

"I serve God."

"What God do you serve?"

"The God that made heaven and earth."

She'd answered the questions in a very rude manner. Her husband shouted out that he thought she was a witch and if she wasn't, she would be one soon.

"Have you seen her do anything?" asked Hathorne.

"No, but she acts badly toward me... It's sad to say, but she's just no good."

Sarah Good had been condemned by her misfortune. Even her husband had to admit he hadn't seen her do anything that would brand her a witch. Prejudice had taken its toll, she would be condemned.

Sarah Osborne was another good choice for the girls to accuse. The town had taken exception to her second marriage. She had married an Irish emigrant whom she'd hired as a farm hand. Now an elderly woman, she had become sick and couldn't attend church. Her lack of attendance was seen as an indication of her guilt. It would be easy to get a conviction. Sarah Osborne's examination follows:

"Who is your familiar?"

"No one."

"Have you made a pact with the Devil?"

"No. I never saw the Devil in my whole life."

"Why are you hurting these children?"

"I'm not hurting them."

"Then who are you getting to hurt them?"

"Nobody."

"How well do you know Sarah Good?"

"Not very well. I haven't even seen her in years."

"When was the last time you saw her?"

"I saw her one day going into town."

"Did you talk to her?"

"No. Except to say, 'How do you do?' I didn't know her name."

"What name did you call her by?"

Sarah Osborne stayed silent for a while. Then she said she'd called her Sarah.

"Sarah Good said that it was you that hurt the children."

"I don't know why the Devil would take on my appearance to go around hurting the children."

The children were brought close to her and asked if she was the one tormenting them. They were asked if she wore the clothes she was wearing at that time when she appeared to them. They all said, "Yes this is one of the women that afflicts us. She wears exactly these clothes when she appears to us."

"I'm more likely to have been bewitched than a witch!" said Sarah Osborne.

"Why do you say that?" asked Hathorne.

"One night, I had been frightened in my sleep and either saw, or dreamed I saw, a black Indian woman, who pinched me on the neck and pulled me by the hair, to the front door of my house."

"Did you ever see anything else?"

"No, and if I did, I wouldn't believe that lying spirit again."

"What lying spirit? Has the Devil ever deceived or lied to you?"

"I don't know the Devil. I've never seen him."

"Then what lying spirit are you talking about?"

"It was a voice I thought I'd heard," said the feeble old woman.

"What did it say to you?"

"That I shouldn't go to church anymore. But I told it that I would go and I did the very next Sabbath day."

"Were you ever tempted again?"

"No."

"Why have you given in to the Devil and not gone to meeting recently?"

"Alas! I have been sick for a long time."

Her husband and some of the other spectators said that she hadn't been to meeting in over three years. It was obvious that the magistrates were pressuring the accused into making wild statements concerning each other and putting false meanings on their answers to trick questions. The hearing was a shoe in for the prosecution. Sarah Osborne was led out of the room and Tituba was brought in. Again Magistrate Hathorne led the questioning.

"Tituba, what evil spirit is your familiar."

"None."

The girls contorted in pain as she answered.

"Why are you hurting these children?"

"I'm not hurting them."

"Then who is?"

"The Devil, for all I know."

"Did you ever see the Devil?"

"He came to me once and asked me to serve him."

With this first admission, the tormented girls stopped their convulsions as if a great weight had been taken off of them.

"Have you seen anyone else."

"I saw four women hurting the children."

The audience stirred at her words. She had seen the torturing of the children. If anyone had doubts about these proceedings, they were dispelled by this woman's testimony.

"Who were they?" The magistrate asked, excitedly.

"Goody (Sarah) Osborne and Sarah Good; I do not know who the others were. Sarah Good and Osborne tried to get me to hurt the children, but I refused. I also saw a tall, white-haired man with a black robe. He seemed to be a gentleman from Boston."

"When did you see them?"

"Last night in Boston."

"What did they say to you?"

"They said, 'Hurt the children.'"

"And did you hurt them?"

"No. The four women and the man hurt them. Then they pounced on me and told me if I didn't hurt the children, they'd hurt me."

"So, did you hurt them."

"Yes, but I won't do it anymore."

"Are you sorry that you hurt them?"

"Yes."

Tituba started to act like she was being afflicted. As her testimony continued her convulsions became more severe.

"Then why are you still hurting them?"

"Because they're telling me to hurt them or they'll do worse things to me."

"What else have you seen?"

"A man came to me and said, 'Serve me.'"

"What kind of service?"

"Hurt the children, and last night they said to 'Kill the children,' and if I didn't do it, they would hurt me more."

"What Apparition do you see?"

"Sometimes it is a hog, and other times it is a large dog. I've seen it four times."

"What does it say to you?"

"The black dog said, 'Serve me,' but I said, 'I'm afraid.' He said if I didn't serve him he would do worse things to me."

"What did you say to that?"

"I will serve you no longer. Then he said he would hurt me. He turned into a man holding a small, yellow bird and threatened to hurt me. He said if I serve him he will give me many pretty things."

"What were those things?"

"He didn't show me what they were."

"What else have you seen?"

"Two cats; a red one and a black one."

"What did they say to you?"

"Serve me."

"When did you see them?"

"Last night, and they said, 'Serve me,' but I said I wouldn't."

"What service?"

"Hurt the children."

"Didn't you pinch Elizabeth Hubbard this morning?"

"The man brought her to me and made me pinch her."

"Why did you go over to Thomas Putnam's and hurt his child?"

"They dragged me over there."

"And what did they want you to do?"

"Kill her with a knife."

A Lieutenant Fuller and some of the other people in the room said that twelve-year-old Ann Putnam Junior had complained about the witches' specters (ghosts) having a knife and that they wanted to cut her head off with it.

"How did you go there?"

"We rode on a stick. Good and Osborne got on behind me and we all held on to each other. We got there very quickly."

"Did you go through the trees or over them?"

"I saw nothing; it was too quick."

"Why didn't you tell your master?"

"I was afraid. They said they would cut my head off if I told anyone."

"Would you have hurt the others if you could?"

"They said they wanted to hurt the others, but they couldn't."

"What familiars did Sarah Good have?"

"She had a little yellow bird. She wanted to give me one."

"What kind of meat did she feed it?"

"She let it suck the blood from between her fingers."

"Did you hurt Mister Curren's child?"

"Goody Good and Goody Osborne told me they hurt Mister Curren's child, and wanted me to hurt him too, but I didn't."

"What did Sarah Osborne have?"

"Yesterday she had a creature that looked like a woman, with two legs and wings."

Abigail blurted out that she'd seen the same creature and that it changed into Goody Osborne.

"What else have you seen with Osborne."

"A hairy thing with a long nose and indescribable face that walks like a man. It had two legs and stands about two or three feet tall. Last night it was standing in front of the fire at Mister Parris's house."

"Didn't you see Sarah Good pounce on Elizabeth Hubbard last Saturday?"

"I saw her set a wolf on her, to afflict her."

The people that were with the maid said that she had complained of a wolf tormenting her. The maid also said that she saw a cat with Sarah Good when she tormented her on another occasion.

"What clothes did the man wear?"

"He wears black clothes. He's a tall man, with white hair, I think."

"How do the women dress?"

"They wear black silk hoods with white silk hoods under them, with topknots. One of them wore a serge coat with a white cap."

"Can you see who's tormenting these children now?"

"Yes, it's Goody Good, she's torturing them in her own shape."

"Who else is hurting them?"

"I'm blind now. I can't see."

If anyone had been of a mind to notice such things, they would have seen the rehearsal that Tituba and the bewitched girls must have had ahead of time. Her answers to the questions coincided precisely with things the girls had told the magistrates and others before the hearing. Obviously Tituba and the girls had set their sights on two other victims, but weren't quite ready to accuse them. They wanted the town to mull over what they'd heard at the hearing first.

Tituba had a convenient lapse of memory concerning who she had seen, naming only Osborne and Good. When it had gotten to the point that she would have to name others, she became "blind." This ignorant slave had a most cunning brain.

The three women were sent to Ipswich jail in the county of Essex, ten miles from the meetinghouse. Heavy metal chains were made to hold them, as it was believed that their specters couldn't leave their bodies if they were restrained. They were examined at three more hearings. Osborne and Good professed their innocence at each hearing. And in each case Tituba said she was guilty and

14

pointed her finger at the others and declared that they were with her doing the Devil's bidding. It should be noted here that Sarah Osborne was old and sickly, the trip back and forth exacted its toll on her little remaining strength.

On March 7, having given them four chances to exonerate themselves, the magistrates sent them to Boston jail to await trial.

Throughout the hearings the tormented children worked their psychological tricks. When one of their so-called tormenters came into the meeting room, they would fall to the floor. Some would become stiff and unmoving, and still others would convulse and bend into strange shapes, moaning and muttering unintelligible sounds. When they were brought up to the accused and made to touch her, their torment would disappear. It was believed that a witch absorbed her spell when she touched her victim. Tituba affected the girls only in the beginning of her first testimony. As soon as she admitted her pact with the Devil, the girls were freed of her specter and she became one of the tormented. As intended, the people in the room felt that she had repented and the Devil was exacting punishment.

Throughout the hearing, Sarah Good and Sarah Osborne had protested their innocence. In light of Tituba's condemning evidence, the people felt that a plea of innocence was an admission of their continuing guilt. This fuzzy logic, of denial proving the person's guilt, was to pervade all the hearings and subsequent trials.

The evidence most acceptable to the magistrates as proof of witchcraft was invisible to them. It was the sighting of the accused person's specter by the afflicted girls, and it was the only evidence that couldn't be disproven.

When the news of the girls' bewitchment first circulated, most people believed it. Martha Corey was one of the rare exceptions. The third wife of Giles Corey, she was an intelligent and pious older woman. She voiced her disbelief openly.

When the first arrests were made and the hearings begun, she became annoyed. She couldn't understand how people were able to be hoodwinked by a bunch of children. The antics of the magistrates infuriated her; she felt they were blinded by their zeal. It was a violation of the Word of God and a lot of silly nonsense. As a good Christian she felt that she could persuade the people of their folly. She would pray often, hoping that God would open the people's eyes to this unrighteous behavior.

As the hearings progressed, a rift developed between her and her husband. Giles had been caught up in the hysteria. Like most people in Salem Village, he attended all the hearings, bringing his distorted views home. Martha lost patience with the man, telling

15

him in no uncertain terms what she thought of him and the others. Several heated discussions ensued, some of them in public places.

One day in a fit of anger she removed her husband's saddle from his horse and hid it. She felt this would prevent him from going into town to attend the hearing. It didn't work. Instead the rift between them grew to ugly proportions.

Martha was a scholar of religion and a prominent member of the church. She was considered one of the most respected and religious people in the area. Sadly, this was exactly what the third victim had to be in order to promote the idea that the Devil had gotten a stranglehold on this small village. If she were accused of being a witch, then no one would be safe from the Devil's grasp.

The townspeople had been allowed to stew in their own juices of distrust, prompted by the knowledge that there were at least two unnamed individuals still tormenting these poor, helpless little children. A rumor was spread around the village that some very religious people were about to be exposed for the witches they were. Martha Corey's name was bandied about as a possible candidate because of her open hostility to the hearings. Her name was picked up by the children. The time was ripe to point the finger.

On March 12, twelve-year-old Ann Putnam Junior complained that several times in the last few days, Martha Corey's specter had tortured and pinched her. Edward Putnam and Ezekiel Cheever went to Thomas Putnam's house and interviewed his daughter. They asked her what Martha had been wearing when her specter came and tortured her. Ann's cunning answer was that she had been struck blind and couldn't see what Martha had been wearing. Neither of the men asked her how she knew that the specter was Martha Corey. Shocked by the little girl's story, they rushed over to Martha's house to further their inquiry.

It is believed that Martha Corey answered the door in some kind of outlandish outfit, probably to make her attire hard to describe. She said, as she opened the door, "I know why you've come here. You want to find out if I'm a witch. Well, I'm not! I can't help the way people talk about me."

Having heard the gossip bandied around the village, she had expected the confrontation with these men. Her next question to them was an assumption of what they would discuss.

"Have you asked my accuser what kind of clothes I was supposed to have worn?"

"Yes, we did. But she told us you'd blinded her so she couldn't see them."

Martha laughed at this. She must have been thinking how clever the little girl had been to come up with that excuse.

"Gentlemen, there aren't any witches. Surely, you don't believe in them?"

The two men talked with her for quite a while, but she wouldn't bend to their accusations. The conversation with Martha, recorded by Cheever, had proved that she was a bright, sensible woman with a freedom of spirit not common for her day. Her religious beliefs were unshakable and of the purest in nature.

The two men returned to Thomas Putnam's house and asked Ann if Martha Corey had visited her while they were gone. Her reply was, "No." To make sure of the accusation, the men invited Martha to come to the Putnam house on March 14. As soon as she walked in the door, Ann became stricken with intense pain. This was all the proof the men needed.

On Saturday, March 19, an arrest warrant was issued. The warrant couldn't be served until Monday, as it was against the law to conduct man's business on the Sabbath. That Sunday, Martha went to church, with the full knowledge of the warrant. She wasn't about to deny her faith for man's silly rules. The other parishioners acted cruelly toward her. They didn't think a sinner, such as she was, had the right to be there.

Monday she was arrested and taken to Nathaniel Ingersoll's house.

CHAPTER III

TWO GOOD WOMEN

March 21, 1692 - March 23, 1692

The examination of Martha Corey took place in the meeting-house on Monday, March 21. It was heavily attended because of her standing in the church. The children, upon seeing Martha became tormented, displaying their best contortions for all to see.

The examination is presented here in its entirety, so that the reader can better understand how the people thought and felt at this pivotal hearing. Mister Hathorne, as was usually the case, conducted the examination.

"You have been arrested. Now tell me why you are tormenting these children?"

"I'm not."

"Then who is doing it?"

"I do not know. Please let me say a prayer."

"We didn't bring you so that you could pray. Why are you hurting them?"

"I am innocent. I have never had anything to do with witch-craft. I'm a God-fearing woman. Please let me pray!"

The children became louder and more spastic.

"Listen to how you're torturing them."

"Oh, God, please let the magistrates see their injustice. God, please show them who is really at fault here."

"Who is hurting these children?"

"I do not know."

"If you are guilty, do you think you can hide it?"

"The Lord knows the truth."

"Tell me what you know about this matter?"

"Why? I'm a God-fearing woman. Do you think I could study witchcraft, too?"

"Then how did you know that the men asked the child what

kind of clothes you wore before they came to see you?"

"One of the men told me."

At this Cheever interrupted saying, "Don't start out with a lie."

Edward Putnam read the notes to her that had been taken at the time. It was quite clear that she'd raised the subject before they did.

"Who told you that?" asked Hathorne.

"He said that the child said it," she said, pointing at Cheever.

"That's a lie," said Cheever.

And it was. The poor old woman had gotten her nine-day-old conversation with the two men all mixed up. But then, she hadn't taken careful notes like they had.

Edward Putnam reread the notes.

"Why did you ask them if the child told them what clothes you wore?" asked Hathorne.

"My husband told me that the other children had told."

"Who told you about the clothes? Why did you ask the men the question?"

"Because I'd heard that the children had told what clothes the others had worn."

"Giles Corey, did you tell her about that?"

"No, Sir. I didn't."

"Didn't you say that your husband had told you?"

She sat in silence. She had been taken aback by her husband's spiteful denial.

"Who is hurting these children. Look at them."

"I can't help them."

"You said you would tell the truth. Why did you ask the question? How did you find out it."

"All I did was ask about it."

"How dare you lie to all these people. You are standing before the law. I expect the truth, like you promised. Now tell me who told you about what clothes had been described?"

"Nobody."

Obviously her outlandish attire had been interpreted to mean that she was hiding whatever clothes she was supposed to have worn when she had afflicted the children.

"How did you know that the children would be asked what clothes you wore?"

"The child would have had to be a genius to know what I had on that day," she said with a smirk.

"I want an answer. You said your husband told you."

"He told me that the children had said that I'd afflicted them."

"How did you know what the men came for? Tell me the truth.

20

How did you know what they came for?"

"I'd heard some talk that the children had said I'd hurt them, and I knew that someone might come to question me."

"But how did you know it?"

"I just knew they would."

"Didn't you say you'd tell the truth? Who told you what they'd come for?"

"Nobody!"

"How did you know?"

"I thought so."

"But you said you knew it."

Some of the children shouted out that a man was whispering in her ear.

"What did the man say to you?"

"You mustn't believe everything these lying children tell you."

"Don't you know what the man whispered?"

"I didn't see anybody."

"Didn't you hear him?"

"No."

The children cried in great pain, falling on the floor and breaking into convulsions.

"If you want mercy from God, you must confess your sins. Do you think you get mercy by increasing your sins?"

"You speak the truth," she said with great piety.

"Look for God's mercy."

"I do."

"Give glory to God and confess."

"But I can't confess. I've done nothing wrong."

"Don't you see how these tormented children charge you?"

"We must not believe liars."

"Didn't you say we were blinded and that you would open our eyes for us?" This question was asked in response to a statement she'd supposedly made to some of the village people.

"Yes, you accuse the innocent."

Part of a document was read to her. It had been written by her step-daughter's husband, Henry Crosby. It claimed that Martha Corey had told him that the accusing girls wouldn't be able to stand up in front of her.

One of the afflicted girls said that Martha's specter had spit at her.

"Why can't the girls stand in front of you?"

"I don't know."

"What do you mean, you don't know?"

"I saw them fall down."

"It seems to me that they're not able to stand up in front of you."

"They can't stand in front of the others."

"But you said they couldn't stand in front of you. Why did you turn on the little girl and spit at her?"

"You believe these children's lies? I saw no spit."

"There are more than two persons that accuse you of witchcraft. How do you plead?"

"I'm innocent."

Mister Hathorne read more of Crosby's document. It stated that even the Devil couldn't stand in front of her.

"What did you mean when you said the Devil couldn't stand in front of you?"

"I didn't say that."

Some of the people in the room claimed they had heard her.

"What can I do? You're all against me!"

"Confess, of course."

"I would if I were guilty."

"These are honest people. What will you say to them? You're a religious woman. Would you lie?"

Abigail Williams cried out, "Next Sunday is Sacrament Day, but she won't be there."

"I don't care."

"You charge the children with lying. One of the things about liars is that they keep changing their story. But the children keep accusing you. This isn't the way of a liar."

"When you're all against me, what can I do?"

"Tell me the truth. Why did you say the magistrates' and ministers' eyes were blinded, and you would open them?"

Martha denied she'd said it and laughed.

"How can we know who's hurting the children, if it's not you?"

"Can an innocent person be guilty?"

"Do you deny these words?"

"Yes."

"Tell us who we're hurting. We came here to catch evildoers. You said you would open our eyes, we are blind."

"You are, if you say I'm a witch."

"You said you would show us."

"No, I didn't."

"Why don't you show us now?"

"I can't. I don't know how."

"What did you strike the maid at Thomas Putnam's with?"

"I never struck anybody in my whole life."

"Two people saw you strike her with an iron rod."

"I didn't do it."

"Then who did? Do you believe the children are bewitched?"

"For all I know, they may be, but I didn't do it."

"You say you're not a witch, maybe you mean you never had a covenant with the Devil. Did you ever make a deal with a familiar?"

"No, never."

"What was that bird the children spoke of?"

"I don't know about any bird."

"You may have decided not to confess, but God knows the truth."

"Yes, he does," she smiled.

"Do you believe you won't be punished?"

"I have nothing to do with witchcraft."

"Why didn't you want your husband to come to the earlier hearings?"

"He came anyway."

"Didn't you take his saddle off his horse?"

"I didn't know why he'd put it on."

"Didn't you know why he'd put it on?"

"I didn't think it would serve any useful purpose."

"Didn't you say you'd open our eyes?"

"Not to find witches."

"Is it a laughing matter to see these children afflicted?"

"No. You're all against me and I can't do anything about it."

"Don't you believe there are witches in the country?"

"I don't know of any."

"Don't you know that Tituba confessed to it?"

"I didn't hear her speak."

"I don't think you'll admit to anything unless we have several witnesses and even then you'll deny it."

She bit her lip and several of the children claimed they were bitten.

"Why did you bite your lip?"

"What's wrong with doing that?"

"What do you say to all these charges?"

"If you're going to hang me, what can I do to stop it?"

"Were you to serve the Devil for ten years?"

"How many?" she laughed. In her laughter she put her hands in the air. When she did several children claimed she pinched them.

"Tell us how the Devil comes in your shape and hurts them. You said you would."

"How can I, how?"

"Why did you say you would show us?"

She laughed again. The interpretation of her statement had been so stupid.

"What book do you want the children to write in?"

"What book? Where would I have a book? I didn't show them one; I didn't have one; I didn't bring one."

The children yelled that a man was whispering in her ear again.

"What book did you take to Mary Walcott?"

"I didn't take any. If the Devil appears in my shape..." She was interrupted by Mister Needham who said that Mister Parker thought she was a witch a long time ago.

"Who is your God?"

"The one that made me."

"What is his name?"

"Jehovah!"

"Do you know him by any other name?"

"God Almighty!!"

"Does the God that you pray to tell you he is God Almighty?"

"I only worship the God who made me."

"How many Gods are there?"

"One."

"How many persons?"

"Three."

"Can't you say there's one God in three blessed persons?" (Sadly her answer was on a fold line and was obliterated with time.).

"Don't you see that the children are normal when your hands are tied?"

The children broke into fits. People in the crowd said she was squeezing her hands together and causing it.

"She just bit her lip," said the marshal. The children broke into pandemonium.

"I believe it is apparent that she is practicing witchcraft among the congregation!" said Reverend Nicholas Noyes of Salem town.

"Why are you hurting them, or is it someone else?"

"I'm not hurting them."

"Why did you say if you're a witch you should get no pardon?"

"Because I am a (pious) woman."

The Reverend Samuel Parris had been the stenographer at the hearing. He had purposefully omitted the word 'pious' from Martha's last answer, putting a blank in its place. Martha was sent directly to Salem jail. She didn't even get a second hearing.

Several interesting facts showed up at the hearing. Martha had made several requests to pray. The magistrates had opened the hearing with a prayer. You can be sure that it had been designed to incense the crowd. If they had let her pray, she would have turned the crowd in her favor. The clergy was afraid of her vast religious knowledge. They had heard her sermons many times before.

She remained silent on a question that would have showed her husband to be a liar. Try as they might, she refused to give out anyone's name that she'd discussed the hearings with for fear that they would be next.

Giles Corey had made a private statement that was never sworn to or finished. It is believed that the magistrates had wanted the eighty-year-old man to give them some evidence to work with. He wouldn't give them the testimony they needed. This might have been the reason that he was later called to task.

The incomplete statement might have had the opposite effect if it had been presented in court, so it was not. It was found among some records in the clerk's office, a disconnected fragment of history.

At about this time, Joseph Parris went over to his brother Samuel's house. He warned him not to let his daughter point the finger at him, or there would be hell to pay. From that time forward, Joseph kept his family well armed, with fresh horses saddled and ready in case of trouble.

The day after Martha Corey had first been accused, March 13, a second name was given out by Ann Putnam Junior. It was the name of a woman that no one would have even thought of considering for anything short of sainthood, Rebecca Nurse. She was a member of the mother church of Salem, a position she never relinquished even though she lived in Salem Village. Being one of the chief matrons, her seat in the Salem Village church was shared with Thomas Putnam Senior's widow. Rebecca was well-known for her kind and gentle ways.

She had, however, picked up a few enemies along the way. The first was Sarah Holton. Several years earlier the Holton's pig had wandered into her garden and uprooted several of her plants. Rebecca had gotten very annoyed and paid a visit to Mister Holton. She sternly read him off for not keeping his pig under control. A few months later Mister Holton died mysteriously. Sarah Holton felt that Rebecca had been the direct cause of her husband's death, although she didn't know how.

Rebecca's second enemy was none other than Ann Putnam Senior, little Ann's mother. The wide rift between them seems to be centered around a group called the "Topsfield Men." Isaac Easty, whose wife was Rebecca Nurse's sister, together with the brothers

Townes, were the leaders of the Topsfield Men.

The Topsfield Men had an ongoing fight with the town over several pieces of land. In the past fifty years, fourteen of Ann Putnam's neighbors and friends had been killed over boundary disputes. Rebecca Nurse's family was strongly opposed to the local party which had existed since the village was founded. Whenever a land dispute came before the council, Rebecca and several family members sided with the Topsfield Men.

On March 23, two things happened. First, Dorcas Good, the five-year-old daughter of Sarah Good, was accused of sending her specter to torture the girls for their having sent her mother to prison.

On that same day, a warrant was issued for Rebecca Nurse. At eight o'clock the following morning, the bed-ridden old woman in her seventies was taken to Nathaniel Ingersoll's. Several charges were lodged against her, four of which were for the detestable practice of witchcraft. These four complaints were lodged by Ann Putnam Junior (12), Mary Walcott (17), Elizabeth Hubbard (17), and Abigail Williams (11). Rebecca was taken to the meetinghouse.

The poor health of the old woman and her status in the community were such that the examination had to be conducted carefully.

Magistrate Hathorne opened the hearing by going over to the four afflicted girls. Approaching one of them he asked, "Tell me, has this woman hurt you?"

"Yes, she beat me this morning."

"Abigail, have you been hurt by this woman?"

"Yes."

Following Abigail's answer, Ann Putnam Junior had a fit. In the midst of this fit she screamed, "Rebecca Nurse is hurting me!"

When it was over, Hathorne asked, "Goody Nurse, Ann Putnam and Abigail Williams complain that you're hurting them. What do you say to that?"

"I can say, before God, that God will vindicate me."

"There's no one here that wants that more than I, but if you're guilty, God will punish you."

A man stood up in the audience. It was Henry Kenney.

"Mister Kenney, what do you have to say?"

"Ever since Rebecca Nurse came in here, I've been having considerable pain."

"It's not only these people that are accusing you, Ann, the wife of Thomas Putnam has also accused you. She said that you have hurt her and led her into temptation."

"I deny it. I haven't even been able to go outside for the last

26

eight or nine days."

Edward Putnam gave evidence that he'd seen the afflictions and heard the girls say that it had been Rebecca Nurse causing them.

"Is this true, Goody Nurse?"

"I've never hurt them or anyone else in my whole life."

"These people accuse you. Is it true?"

"No!"

"Are you innocent of witchcraft?"

He was beginning to have his doubts about her guilt. Ann Putnam Senior jumped up from the crowd, interrupting Rebecca's answer.

"Didn't you bring the man in black with you, and ask me to tempt God and die? How often have you celebrated your own damnation?" she screamed vehemently.

The room was in shock from this grown woman's outburst. Even Rebecca hadn't expected it. Ann Putnam Senior had added her name to the list of the bewitched.

Rebecca Nurse raised her hands in the air and said, "Oh, Lord, help me!"

As soon as her hands had raised, the children had terrible fits.

"Don't you see what's happening to these children? As soon as your arms are loose, you afflict them," said Hathorne.

Mary Walcott and Elizabeth Hubbard got up and came over to Rebecca saying, "She is the one whose specter tortures and afflicts us!"

"Now these two grown women accuse you. What do you say? Don't you see them and hear them accuse you?"

"The Lord knows that I haven't hurt them. I am an innocent person!"

"It's horrible to see all this agony. Most of the people here have wept openly. Yet, you, an educated woman, being charged with consorting with the Devil, haven't shed a tear."

"You don't know what's in my heart!"

"You would do well, if you are guilty, to confess and give glory to God."

"I'm as innocent as a newborn baby."

"I don't know much about apparitions, but it bothers me that you have been charged with having a familiar spirit. They say that you have a familiar spirit that comes to you. What do you say to that?"

"I don't have one, Sir!"

"If you have one, confess and give glory to God. I pray that if you are innocent, God clears you. And if you are guilty that God punishes you. Give me an honest answer. Have you a familiarity with spirits?"

"No! I only have familiarity with God!"

"How did you become sick? There is a lot of gossip concerning this matter."

"I have a weak stomach."

"Don't you have some wounds?"

"All my sickness and pains are the natural effects of many years. It's my old age."

"You don't know, if you have a pact with the Devil. Now, you are here listening to these people. Tell us that a man in black is whispering in your ear and birds are all around you. What do you say to that?"

"It's a lie! I am innocent."

"Possibly, you may not think you are a witch, but haven't you been tempted to become one?"

"I have not!"

"What a sad thing it is that a local church member and now a second church member from Salem, should be brought here on such charges," said Hathorne.

A middle-aged woman by the name of Gertrude Pope had a violent fit. A few days earlier, Gertrude Pope had caused quite a commotion at Martha Corey's hearing. All the hearings had caused her to have a nervous breakdown and she became obsessed with the idea that the accused was tormenting her. She had become violent and thrown a couple of things at the poor woman. One of the items, a shoe, hit Martha, squarely on the head, knocking her down. Her temporary insanity would eventually leave her and she would strongly denounce the witch trials in later months.

All the other allegedly afflicted in the room broke out in loud groans and cries of pain. The sounds they made, could be heard a block away and the convulsions were so horrible that even the strongest person was moved by them.

"Tell me, haven't you ever had anything unnatural appear to you?"

"Not now or ever in my entire life."

"Do you think they are suffering voluntarily or involuntarily?"

"I can't tell you."

"That's strange, everyone else knows."

"I mustn't say anything."

"They are accusing you of hurting them. If you think they are doing it on purpose you must think of them as murderers."

"I don't know what to think of it."

"Then you are calling them murderers and I so charge you."

"All I said was that I didn't know what to think of them. I am quite hard of hearing and don't hear the whole of some of your questions."

"Do you think these children suffer against their wills or not? Give me an answer."

"I don't think they suffer against their wills!"

"Why didn't you ever visit these afflicted persons?"

"Because, I was afraid I would get fits too."

The children started having fits in accordance with her body movements.

"Tell me why, when you are examined, the children have fits?"

"I've got nobody to answer to but God!" she said as she raised her hand in reverence.

The children broke into tormented rage.

"Do you think these people are bewitched?"

"I think they are."

"When witchcraft was first brought out in the open there was no suspicion of Tituba, Mister Parris's Indian woman. She claimed much love for their daughter Elizabeth, yet it was Tituba's specter that tortured her. Why shouldn't you be guilty too, since your specter is torturing these people?"

"Would you have me make myself a liar?"

At this time Rebecca's head drooped to one side. The four girls mimicked her, sending a shockwave through the room. Elizabeth Hubbard's neck froze in the position and Abigail yelled, "Straighten Goody Nurse's head or the maid's neck will break." Some people held Rebecca's head up and Elizabeth immediately straightened hers.

The magistrates asked Mister Parris to read the deposition he'd taken while Ann Putnam Senior was having one of her fits. After he had finished, Hathorne asked the final question, "What do you think of this?"

"I can't help it if the Devil appears in my shape."

That day, Ann Putnam Senior had made quite a commotion with her fits. The magistrates had to let her husband take her home. Her impression on the people swayed their judgment in favor of finding Rebecca guilty. Rebecca was sent to Salem jail to await trial.

The next hearing was held immediately after Rebecca Nurse. It concerned the little girl, Dorcas Good. Her age was not established for certain, but most believe it was between four and five. The marshal was ashamed to bring her in so he had one of his deputies, Samuel Brabrook, do it. The deputy carried the poor little waif in and set her on the podium. Her three accusers were Ann

Putnam Junior, Mary Walcott and Mercy Lewis (19).

The three girls charged that little Dorcas had bitten them, showing everyone the little teeth marks on their arms. Then they claimed that she pinched and almost choked them to death. Ann and Mary had the usual demonstration of fits for the audience.

At times the girls would complain that Dorcas was hurting them and point to different areas of their bodies. Upon examination of the areas, small pins were discovered. This was considered absolute proof of Dorcas's guilt. Charged with witchcraft, she was sent to Salem jail to await trial with her mother. She spent several months in chained confinement. On December 10, 1692, bail in the amount of 50 pounds was paid for her release. The man who paid the bail was Samuel Ray, a member of the Massachusetts Bay Council. Eighteen years later, in a petition for restitution, her father William told the court that among the sufferings of his family, "A child of four or five years old was in prison seven or eight months and, being chained in the dungeon, was so badly used and terrified that she hath ever since been very chargeable, having little or no reason to govern herself." Little Dorcas never recovered from her frightening ordeal.

A few days previous to all of this, Salem Village had a new resident. His name was Deodat Lawson. Some years before, he had been the village's minister. His wife and child had met with untimely deaths and he had moved away. He took up residence in Nathaniel Ingersoll's house. He was exposed to the girls' shenanigans almost as soon as he'd arrived. Mary Walcott brought the act right to his door. After his exposure to this girl's torment, he wanted to find out more, so he went to Mister Parris's house.

Abigail gave him a terrifying show. She ran through the house throwing burning sticks around and running to the chimney as if she wanted to fly up the middle. The minister studied these girls closely.

In the days that followed, the girls hinted to him in their fits that the people that had been responsible for his wife and daughter's death were the very ones being arrested at this time. He felt that there was probably some truth in what they said, and decided to delve into the matter and see what he could do to help in the hearings.

Deodat Lawson was in attendance when Ann Putnam Senior had one of her seizures. [Author's note: I say seizure because the described symptoms were the same as an epileptic fit. It is quite possible that Ann mistook this natural occurrence for bewitchment and picked out her longtime enemies.] She had just come out of one when he arrived. Her husband asked if he would pray with them, which he did. During the prayer Ann had another seizure. She stiffened up and froze into a grotesque position and remained silent for quite a while. When it looked like she might be coming around, her husband took her off the bed and tried to bend her still-stiff knees. Eventually she was able to bend them and finish her prayer. When she was fully conscious, she didn't remember what had happened. Deodat was struck with horror at what he had seen.

The next morning Deodat Lawson went to Rebecca Nurse's hearing. He didn't stay for the whole thing. He had to finish his sermon for a special service being held that very afternoon. It was to be a sermon of great historical significance.

CHAPTER IV

SATAN'S ACCURSED LEGIONS

March 23, 1692 - April 19, 1692

The meeting hall and its surrounding grounds were swarming with people. They had come from all the surrounding areas to hear Deodat Lawson's sermon.

The length and vast Biblical content of the sermon would indicate, even to the layman, that it must have been written weeks before Lawson arrived in Salem Village. He had no free time from the time he arrived until that fateful afternoon. He'd spent almost every waking hour visiting the afflicted children and attending the village meetings.

It was probably no accident that the sermon was to take place after the hearings of Martha Corey and Rebecca Nurse. Doesn't it seem strange that arrest warrants for the two pious women took so long to be issued and then the hearings were held after Deodat Lawson's arrival? What better time to tell the people that the Devil had infiltrated their ranks than after their most pious and respected women had been proved witches? If Martha Corey had been vindicated, the sermon might not have been given, or if it had, the results wouldn't have been so extreme.

The sermon was, as I said earlier, extremely long, and rather than bore the reader, I will touch on its three main discourses. Every passage in the Bible concerning the Devil's possession of man, and every passage of man's final battle with the Devil seems to have been included, along with Lawson's skillful interpretations.

First and foremost, the point was stressed that the Devil had taken over Salem Village and was going to devour it in sin. Demons from within would destroy even the most pious and use them to do his bidding. From there the Devil's legions would branch out and devour the world. (See Revelations 12:12, as an example.)

33

Next, he pointed out what God wanted the people to do. He said that they had been chosen to fight the battle of battles. Their small village was the place where Satan was to be fought for the last time. Victory would destroy him; defeat would damn the world. They were God's chosen army.

Anything that had been done so far, or was going to be done to bring witches to task, was justified by a piece of scripture coupled with Lawson's interpretation. He even came up with an excuse for the children, in case it was discovered that they had been lying. Searching out and destroying witches was mandatory to all good Christians; their immortal souls depended on it.

His third discourse was indicative of considerable foresight and contained a touch of brilliance. He must have figured on the possibility that he might be wrong. So it was impressed upon the crowd that it would be ungodly to take revenge on one another if someone should be wrongly accused. Forgiveness of mistakes, whether caused by tricks of the Devil or acts of God, was a sign of piety. Vengeance was a condemnation to the fiery pit.

The sermon stirred the people to a fever pitch. The witch hunt was on! People that had done some questionable things in the past few months started to get guilty complexes.

The next day, March 25, Mary Sibley went to Mister Parris's house. She had become worried about her actions in the early stages of the girls' bewitchments. At that time, she had suggested that John Indian make a witch cake to discover if the girls were possessed. The suggestion was accepted. A witch cake was made by taking some cake batter and mixing it with the afflicted girl's urine. The finished cake was fed to a dog. The idea had been that the dog would have fits just like the girls if indeed they were possessed. Mister Parris voiced his disapproval at the time, saying that it was blasphemous to use a witch's method to catch a witch.

Parris wrote out a document confessing Mary's sin and asking forgiveness. Some of the wording of the confession took the blame for the things that happened later. Another part stated that the witch's cake had opened the door to the gates of hell, releasing the evil one. Mister Parris handed it to Mary and she signed it.

One of the original founders of the village church was a man by the name of Peter Cloyse (52). He was a man of good character and high standing in the community. A few years back he'd married a widow by the name of Sarah Bridges (50). Sarah's sister was none other than Rebecca Nurse.

When they'd heard about the charges brought against Rebecca, they were astonished. The verdict of the hearing upset Sarah a great deal.

Sunday, March 27, was Sacrament Day. Sarah and Peter were devout Christians. She was so upset with the verdict that she didn't want to go to church. Peter tried to convince her that it would be a sin to miss communion. Reluctantly she agreed to go.

Having not wanted to come to church in the first place, she was ill-prepared for the many references to the goings on of the previous week. When Mister Parris got up to read his choice of scripture, aimed by inference directly at her sister, she'd had enough. Fuming, Sarah got up and walked abruptly out of the church. Not much notice of this event would have been taken, if it hadn't been for a freak incident. As she went out the door, it slammed behind her. A breeze had come in through the open windows slamming the door. It appeared to many as a sign of God's displeasure with her.

Before communion, Mister Parris read Mary Sibley's signed confession. Asked if she had so sinned, and if she was truly sorry, Mary said yes. It was unanimously agreed to accept her confession.

Samuel Sibley, Mary's husband, was the uncle of Mary Walcott, one of the bewitched children. It had become an unwritten law not to cast doubt on members of the afflicted children's families. Because of this, Mary wasn't accused of being a witch. Mary's family connections were enormous and if anyone had tried to do anything to her at this time, there would have been wide repercussions. Instead, her confession served to show the public that they would be found out and punished if they tried to meddle with the afflicted or in any way tried to cast the demon out. Mister Parris had set himself up as their savior, the only one who had the right to fight this evil.

The previous week had removed all common sense and reason from the villagers' minds. On Monday, March 28, at Ingersoll's tavern, one of the afflicted girls pointed at the rafters and said, "Old witch! I'll have her hang!" She claimed that it was the specter of John Proctor's wife, Elizabeth.

"You're a liar, I don't see anything!" said William Rayment (26).

"I was only kidding," said the girl, embarrassed.

John Proctor had disliked the hearings from the beginning and made his opinion known to anyone that would listen. The day after Rebecca Nurse's hearing, he had said, "If we let these girls go unchecked, we'll all be branded devils and witches!"

One of the afflicted girls was his maid servant, Mary Warren. When he'd taken as much of her goings-on as he could, he had her sit down and use his spinning wheel. He told her that if she got up from it, he would whip her. Her fits disappeared. He was of the opinion that a good thrashing would stop the other's from carrying on their nonsense as well. When Mister Parris's servant, John Indian, became afflicted, John Proctor went over to the Parris' household and asked that they give the man to him. He said he'd beat it out of him just as he had his maid servant. Needless to say, Mister Parris was furious at his interference.

Several of the townspeople had mentioned Elizabeth Proctor's name around the afflicted girls, so they happily picked her as one of their next victims.

On Monday, April 4, Jonathan Walcott and Nathaniel Ingersoll, now calling themselves Captain and Lieutenant respectively, presented two complaints to the Magistrates Hathorne and Corwin. The complaints were against Elizabeth Proctor and Sarah Cloyse, for "various charges concerning witchcraft."

On or about Tuesday, April 5, Sarah Good gave birth to a child in Boston jail. The child soon died from the poor conditions that existed there. Unbaptized, it died without a name.

The colony of Massachusetts was in a state of turmoil from an entirely unrelated matter: Massachusetts' charter had been suspended in 1689. The people didn't want to be a colony of England; they wanted to be a royal province. The royal governor had been imprisoned and the governor they'd had before becoming a colony was put back in office. His name was Simon Bradstreet and at the time he was placed back in office, he was 87 years old. For three years the people lived completely independent of England.

Sir William Phips was sent to England to obtain a new charter which had been negotiated by the Reverend Increase Mather. He was due to return in May of 1692. Until his return, no legal proceedings could take place; there was no court system.

Governor Bradstreet had always opposed the small witch trials of the past, but his age prevented his getting involved in this new situation. If things hadn't happened so quickly, he might have been able to prevent the outcome. On the other hand, his deputy governor, Thomas Danforth, had pursued witches in other towns before Salem Village even thought of doing it. Needless to say he zealously jumped at the chance to do something.

Danforth received messages from the magistrates in Salem Village concerning the new arrests. He wanted to be in on the situation, so on April 8, he sent a warrant down to them, asking that the prisoners be delivered to Salem the following Monday, April 11.

John Proctor loved his wife. He accompanied her to the hearing in order to give her confidence and moral support. The meeting hall in Salem was much larger than the one in Salem Village. When the accused walked inside, they were amazed by the great throng of people. Sitting at the back of the room weren't the two magistrates they had expected, but a council of several people. Heading the council was the deputy governor, Thomas Danforth. The other members of the council consisted of Jonathan Hathorne, Jonathan Corwin, James Russell of Charleston, Major Samuel Appleton of Ipswich, Isaac Addington, and Captain Samuel Sewall, both of Boston. Samuel Parris was there at his own request; he wanted to record the proceedings.

This wasn't to be the simple preliminary hearing the people of Salem Village were used to. Someone had decided to turn it into a hearing by tribunal, similar to another dark part of the history of man, the Inquisition. The women sat down and the hearing was begun. Although Parris wasn't there officially, he was the one that asked the questions for the magistrates, as they were not familiar with the case. John Indian was the first person examined.

"John, who hurt you?"

"First Goody Proctor, and then Goody Cloyse."

"What did she do to you?"

"She brought me the book to sign."

"John, tell the truth. Who hurts you?"

"The first one was a lady."

"Who next?"

"Goody Cloyse."

"But who hurt you next?"

"Goody Proctor."

"What did she do to you?"

"She choked me and brought me the book."

"How often did she come and torment you?"

"Many times, both her and Goody Cloyse."

"Do they come to you at night as well as in the day?"

"They come mostly during the day."

"Who?"

"Goody Cloyse and Goody Proctor."

"Where did she grab you?"

"At my throat to choke me."

"Do you know Goody Cloyse and Goody Proctor?"

"Yes. This is Goody Cloyse," he said, as he pointed his finger at her.

"When did I hurt you?" yelled Sarah Cloyse.

"A great many times."

"Oh, you're a big liar!"

"What did Goody Cloyse do to you?" asked the court.

"She bit and pinched me until I bled."

"When was the last time this woman hurt you?"

"Yesterday morning at church."

"Were there any times before that?"

"Yes. Very many times."

"Mary Walcott, who's hurting you?"

"Goody Cloyse."

"What did she do to you?"

"She hurt me."

"Did she bring the book?"

"Yes."

"What were you supposed to do with it?"

"To touch it and be cured," she said, as she fell to the floor and had a fit. She was picked up and carried over to Sarah Cloyse, who was made to touch her. As soon as she did the afflicted girl returned to normal and the proceedings continued.

"Does she come alone?"

"Sometimes alone and sometimes with Goody Nurse and Goody Corey, and lots of others I don't know." She fell into another fit and was once again cured when she touched Sarah. Her testimony was finished and she went and sat with the others.

"Abigail Williams, did you see the large group of people that came to eat and drink at Mister Parris's house?"

"Yes, sir. That was for their sacrament."

"How many were there?"

"About forty. Goody Cloyse and Goody Good were their demons."

"What was the sacrament?"

"They said it was our blood. They had it twice a day."

He turned to Mary Walcott, "Have you seen a white man?"

"Yes, sir, very many times."

"What sort of man was he?"

"A fine stern man. When he came, he made all the witches tremble."

"I saw the man at Deacon Ingersoll's," said Abigail.

"Who was at Deacon Ingersoll's when he was there?"

"Goody Cloyse, Goody Nurse, Goody Corey and Goody Good."

Sarah Cloyse asked for a drink of water. After she received it she fainted. The pressure of the lies and the accusations had gotten to her. The children broke into horrible fits, saying that her specter had gone off to prison to visit her sister, Rebecca. The people rushed to the children and carried them over to touch her. No one seemed the least concerned about Sarah.

When the hearing was resumed, Elizabeth Proctor was

brought forward. Her husband's love for her was very apparent, as he stepped forward to be by her side. A strong man of great devotion, he had made up his mind to protect her with his life if necessary.

"Elizabeth Proctor, you understand that you have been charged with various acts of witchcraft. How do you plead? Tell the truth, unless you want to be afflicted. You must speak the truth, as you will answer to God... Mary Walcott, does this woman hurt you?"

"I never saw her for her to hurt me."

"Mercy Lewis, does she hurt you?"

The girl opened her mouth as if to say something, but nothing came out.

"Ann Putnam Junior, does she hurt you?"

Ann couldn't speak either.

"Abigail Williams, does she hurt you?"

Abigail had her hand stuffed into her mouth.

"John Indian, does she hurt you?"

"This was the woman that came in her nightgown and choked me."

"Did she ever bring you the book?"

"Yes, sir."

"What were you supposed to do?"

"Write in it."

"What? This woman?"

"Yes, Sir!"

"Are you sure it was her?"

"Yes, Sir."

He asked Abigail and Ann the questions again, but they still couldn't answer.

"What do you say, Goody Proctor, to these things?"

"As God is my witness, I know nothing of it. I'm as innocent as a newborn baby."

"Ann Putnam Junior, does this woman hurt you?"

This time she answered, "Yes, Sir, very many times."

Elizabeth Proctor looked toward her accusers, prompting them to have fits.

"She doesn't bring the book to you, does she?"

"Yes, sir, many times. She says she made her maid sign it."

"Abigail Williams, does this woman hurt you?"

"Yes, sir, often."

"Does she bring the book to you?"

"Yes."

"What does she want you to do with it?"

"To write in it and I will be cured."

Looking at Elizabeth, Abigail asked, "Didn't you tell me that your maid wrote her name in the book?"

Her statement accused Mary Warren, the afflicted maid servant that John Proctor had claimed to have "cured," of signing a pact with the Devil.

"Dear child, it's not so. There's another judgment, dear child." she said, sweetly.

Abigail and Ann had another fit. When they came out of them, one of them pointed toward the ceiling and shouted, "Look! There's Goody Proctor standing on a beam!" Both girls acted as if they could see her plainly. The audience looked but saw nothing. John Proctor must have said something in the heat of the moment about the girls' honesty. In the next instant they were accusing him of hurting them. Within seconds the other afflicted persons chimed in claiming he was hurting them too.

"Ann Putnam, who is hurting you?"

"Mister Proctor and his wife is, too."

One of the afflicted yelled, "There's Mister Proctor picking up Misses Pope's feet!" Her feet went up into the air.

"What do you say to these things Mister Proctor?"

"I don't know! I'm innocent!"

Abigail Williams yelled, "There's Mister Proctor going up to Misses Pope." Misses Pope fell to the floor in a fit. Then she hollered out again, "There's Mister Proctor, he's going to hurt Goody Bibber!" and Sarah Bibber (36) fell into a fit.

Hysteria hit the crowd, accusations were flying everywhere.

Benjamin Gould, a man not related to the afflicted gave testimony that he had seen Giles Corey and his wife Martha, John Proctor and his wife Elizabeth, Sarah Cloyse, Rebecca Nurse, and Misses Griggs in his bedroom last Thursday night. One of the afflicted children, Elizabeth Hubbard, was in a trance for the whole hearing. If she had been awake she would have heard her aunt's name (Griggs) when it had been spoken.

Mister Gould had added two names to the list of witches. His mention of Giles Corey annoyed the officials. They weren't quite ready to arrest him yet. The second name, Misses Griggs, the wife of Doctor Griggs, was brought up before it was felt prudent to accuse any of the afflicted's relatives. They didn't want to make any waves or they might jeopardize the trials to come.

The hearing was adjourned until the next morning, at which time Mister Parris submitted further evidence against John Proctor. The ruling was that there was sufficient evidence to hold them for trial. John Proctor, Elizabeth Proctor, and Sara Cloyse were taken to Boston jail, together with Rebecca Nurse, Martha Corey, and little Dorcas Good.

The hearing had gone well. The men who had sat on the council believed in earnest that they had done the right thing. Acting was forbidden in the Puritan faith. No one had ever seen a performance of any kind. If they had, the afflicted people would have been spotted for what they were. Instead, the observers assumed that what the afflicted were doing had to be real. When a touch from one of the accused made the afflicted individual normal, that person had to be a witch; there was no other explanation.

The girls had practiced their roles for several months before making them public. They had even entertained people in their own households long before the fits were taken seriously. The older people that were starting to appear with them had been caught up in the general hysteria. If a person walked into the hearing and developed a stomach cramp, he had every right to assume that one of the accused had given it to him.

Note that Samuel Parris's nine-year-old daughter, Elizabeth, has disappeared from the limelight. Once the first hearings had gotten under way, she was shuffled off somewhere. Could it be that her father knew the truth and wanted to protect her from the repercussions? Even the Reverend Lawson didn't mention meeting her, only Abigail, Parris's niece.

The hearing had changed the way witchcraft was looked at. In the beginning it was a Salem Village affair. The hearing in Salem Town was conducted by the ruling government. That made it a Massachusetts problem. If it had been left at the local level, the problem would have died as it had many times before. But now word spread everywhere. After this splashy hearing, the hearings were transferred back to Salem Village with the original two magistrates presiding.

As was mentioned earlier, Mary Warren had been accused of signing the Devil's book. It was not in the girls' best interests to accuse one of their own. Mary had been an active member of the girls' "circle" from the beginning. They had met many times at both Mister Putnam's and Mister Parris's house. The only reason she would be accused that makes any sense is because it would be of some benefit to her and her friends. Whatever the motive, she broke away from the others and started to bad mouth them publicly. In a short amount of time, the other girls accused her of witchcraft.

Arrest warrants were issued on April 18 for Bridget Bishop of Salem, Giles Corey and Mary Warren of Salem Farms, and Abigail Hobbs of Topsfield. The four were taken to Nathaniel Ingersoll's.

They were to have their hearing in Salem Village at eight the next morning.

Mary was put in with four prisoners charged with the same crime she'd been charged with. She made it a point to let everyone around her know what she thought of her former friends. Mary would go on and on about how anyone that would listen to the afflicted girls might as well interview a crazy person and use that information for the hearings. She claimed that she had been sick and had seen several people's specter. As soon as she recovered, the visions were gone. Her fellow prisoners wrote a deposition against her, repeating what they had heard her say.

The Salem Village hearings were still being run by Hathorne and Corwin. Mary Warren walked into the meeting room. As soon as she entered, the girls fell to the floor in fits.

"Mary Warren, you stand here accused of various charges of witchcraft. What have you got to say for yourself? Are you guilty or not?"

"I am innocent."

"Has she hurt you?" Hathorne asked the afflicted girls. Only one of the girls could speak. Betty Hubbard said, "Yes," and fell into a fit.

"Not too long ago you were an afflicted person; now you are doing the afflicting. How did this happen?"

"I look up to God and thank God for his great mercy."

"What! Do you think it is merciful to hurt others?"

The girls moaned and squirmed in pain. Soon Misses Pope and John Indian joined in.

Suddenly, Mary Warren fell down, rolling head over heels as if struck from behind, in a violent fit of her own. The girls yelled, "She was going to confess, but the specters of Giles Corey, John Proctor and his wife just came, told her not to confess, and struck her down." (How's that for evidence of a conspiracy?)

Her fit continued for quite a while. At one point she claimed that she was deaf and blind. When she'd recovered she spoke.

"I will speak ... Oh, I am sorry for it! I am sorry for it!" Squeezing her hands together she fell into another fit. When she recovered she tried to speak, but her teeth clenched together and she had another fit saying, "Oh, Lord, help me! Oh, good Lord, save me!" She came to again.

"I will tell! I will tell!" And another fit.

"I will tell, they did, they did, they did." Another fit.

"I will tell, I will tell! They brought me to it!" Another fit.

She was taken out of the meeting room and allowed to rest. (Bridget Bishop's hearing was next and will be skipped for now, so that I may finish Mary's story.)

After Bridget's hearing, Mary was brought back in. Once again she was struck by fits. When they subsided the questioning continued.

"Did you sign the Devil's book?"

"No!"

"Have you touched it?"

"No!"

More fits ensued. She was taken outside for a breath of fresh air. After a long period of time had passed, she was brought back in. She was immediately struck with fits, so they sent her away.

When the day's hearings were over, the magistrates sent for Mary to be brought to their chambers. She was interviewed by the magistrates and ministers.

"I won't say a thing ... But I will, I will speak, Satan! She said she will kill me. Oh! She said she'll get me for this and claw me to death. Avoid Satan! In the name of God, avoid!" She fell into yet another fit saying, "Will you? I will stop you, in the name of God!"

When she came out of it, the magistrate asked, "Tell us how far have you given in to him?"

She had another fit.

"What did you say you should do, to make you well?"

She bit her lip so she couldn't speak. The magistrates sent her back to her cell.

She played this game of tag with the magistrates into the middle of May. Then she broke away from Satan and told all. She wrecked havoc and death in every direction with her false accusations. She was released from Salem jail, which wasn't the normal practice for a confessed witch. She testified against ten individuals, and seven of them were put to death. It is believed that she had a hand in convicting several others, but the records have been lost.

43

CHAPTER V

THREE BISHOPS

April 19,1692 - May 3,1692

Bridget Bishop's hearing took place in the middle of Mary Warren's. Bridget was a woman of questionable reputation by her time's moral standards. She had been accused of witchcraft by a neighbor, in 1678, but the charges were eventually dropped. With her many parties and stylish, brightly-colored clothing, her life-style was flamboyant. When her name was mentioned as being a witch, no one was really surprised. Some felt relieved that she would finally be stopped from corrupting the youths in the area.

Several of the people from Salem Town testified against her.

As she was led into the meeting room, the afflicted children's usual ruckus took place. She asked the people in the room to bear witness to her innocence. Hathorne read the charges against her. Then he started his interrogation with a question concerning the types of witchcraft she practiced.

"I swear to all of you that I am innocent."

"Has this women hurt you?"

"Yes," the children answered, punctuating their answers with fits.

"You are being accused by four or five of the people here. What do you have to say about it?"

Bridget was not a Salem Village resident. She was from Salem, and the many faces in the room were complete strangers to her.

"I never saw these people before, nor have I ever been here before. I never hurt them in my life."

"Bridget Bishop's specter is over there. There she is!" shouted one of the people in the room, pointing to a particular spot. Jonathan Walcott, Mary Walcott's brother, drew his sword and struck at the invisible form.

Mary screamed,"You've hit her; you've torn her coat. I heard it tear."

"Is your coat cut?" Hathorne asked Bridget.

"No!"

An examination of Bridget Bishop's clothing revealed two cuts in the fabric. But they didn't appear to be the cuts that a sword would make. Jonathan Walcott's quick thinking answer to this was, "The sword was still in it's scabbard when I struck." The magistrates accepted his explanation.

Information had been provided to the magistrates of Bridget's activities in Salem. Hathorne questioned her on these matters.

"They say you bewitched your first husband until he died."

"If it please, Your Worship, I know nothing about it."

"What do you say to these murders that you've been accused of?"

"I hope I'm not guilty of murder! I got nobody to look to (for help), but God," she said, as she raised her eyes heavenward.

The afflicted girls imitated her actions, locking their eyes in upward slants. Soon they had all become stricken with fits.

"Don't you see how they are tormented? Are you practicing witchcraft in front of us? What do you say to this? Don't you have the heart to confess?"

"I am innocent. I know nothing about it. I am not a witch. I don't know what a witch is," she said calmly.

"She tried to get us to sign the Devil's book!" said the children.

Bridget shook her head. She was a little bewildered that these children, whom she'd never seen before, were making such an accusation. She stuck valiantly to her denials throughout the hearing. At the close of her hearing she said, "I don't know whether there are witches or not."

On her way to the village jail around the corner, she expressed her lack of feelings for the children, one way or the other.

Giles Corey had brutally murdered one of his servants in 1675. From that time on, he had established himself as a man to be feared. In late 1691, he headed the anti-Parris movement. This didn't exactly endear him to the Parris household. Since his wife's imprisonment, he had become regretful of his actions against her. He had turned a family quarrel into a major calamity. Now he was facing the same charge as her, and there was little doubt that his enemies would condemn him.

The hearing opened in the usual manner, with the girls having their fits and hurling their accusations. The afflicted complained so much about his pinching them that his hands were ordered held in place. The magistrates, loosing their tempers, yelled, "Isn't it more than enough to practice witchcraft in other places? Must you do it now, in front of the court?"

"I am a poor creature and can't help it!"

The children started to mimic his motions. The magistrates became more irritated.

"Why do you tell such wicked lies in front of witnesses?"

One of Giles' hands was released and immediately the girls had tremendous fits. They followed every move he made. When he sucked in his cheeks the girls did the same. His accusers tried to make out that his fighting with his wife had been a long-term thing. He insisted that the hearings had been the only thing on which they had disagreed.

Sarah Bibber accused Giles of calling her husband a devil and lapsed into a fit. When she came out of it, she said that one time he had said he'd seen the Devil in the shape of a big black dog, and he had been afraid. Corey heard nothing but the words that he had been afraid. This blinded him to the proceedings. He felt that he was afraid of nothing and let his temper get the better of him. He vehemently denied it.

"What did you see in the barn? Why do you deny it?"

"I saw nothing but my cattle!"

Several people said that he'd been afraid of what he'd seen.

"Well! What do you say to these witnesses? What was it that frightened you?"

"I don't think I've spoken that word in my entire life!" His son said that his father was going to commit suicide and blame it on him. Suicide was a crime against the Bible, so the magistrates charged him with the crime of attempted suicide. He was at a loss for what to do - even his sons-in-law testified against him. He was taken around the corner to the village jail.

Abigail Hobbs was one of those people that lives apart from society. She was at best antisocial. Rude and a derelict, she wandered through the woods at strange hours and slept under the trees - something that a sane woman wouldn't think of doing. One day, while visiting some of her mother's friends, she came into the room and said that her mother wasn't baptized. In front of everyone, she threw water in her mother's face and baptized her. She was for all intents and purposes an insane woman. Her hearing had probably been the first one that day, but the telling of it has been saved till last.

There were two charges against her. The first was for making a covenant with the Devil at Casco Bay in 1688. This was considered to be of grave importance, as it indicated that witchcraft had spread to neighboring communities. The second charge was practicing witchcraft against the afflicted girls at Salem Village in 1692.

In spite of her insanity, she had enough foresight to confess that she was indeed a witch. To put it into her own words, she said, "I sold myself body and soul to the Old Boy!"

She told the magistrates about the beings that came to her and asked her to sign the book. She claimed that they had promised her some pretty clothes if she did.

"And did you sign the book?"

"Yes, sir. I did."

"Where is the clothing they promised?"

"I never got it."

She had a large hand in proving that the girls were being honest in their accusations. The afflicted girls were silent throughout her hearing. This convinced the magistrates that she was truly repentant.

Her confession stirred up momentum in the proceedings. She went on to name several other people that she claimed were also witches. Included among those named were her own mother and father. The afflicted girls picked up on the names she threw out, and by the next day a whole new rash of accusations appeared on the scene.

On April 20, when the magistrates visited her in her cell, she told them about her involvement in the Satanic rights; how she and the other worshipers ate the blood-soaked bread and drank the wine of the Devil.

Giles Corey, Bridget Bishop, Mary Warren and Abigail Hobbs were sent to prison for trial.

On April 21, arrest warrants were issued and nine persons were arrested. On April 22, they were brought to the meetinghouse in Salem Village for a hearing. These arrests were a direct result of Abigail Hobbs's testimony.

The hearings had taken on a more sinister approach. The prisoner now stood about eight feet from the magistrates bench. The afflicted girls were placed between the accused and the magistrates. A constable held the prisoner's hands and the prisoner was ordered to look at the magistrates only. After the hearing the prisoner was asked to recite the Lord's Prayer. It was believed that a witch couldn't recite it without mispronouncing one of the words. Giving each prisoner this knowledge assured them of at least one nervous stumble.

William and Deliverance Hobbs were Abigail's parents. Deliverance didn't have a very strong character. Because of this, she broke down under questioning and said she would admit to anything the magistrates wanted her to. This destroyed any chance her husband may have had at his hearing. But he defended himself valiantly in spite of it. His laxity in going to church was deemed evidence against him.

Two men told the magistrates that William left the room whenever his family read the Scriptures. He flatly denied it. The men said that his daughter had told them so. Steadfast, he answered every question with the conviction of an honest man. It made no difference, he was bound over for trial and sent to prison.

William Hobbs's trial was not as quick in coming as some of the others in this horrifying tale. Somehow on December 14, two of his close neighbors and friends, John Nichols and Joseph Towne, bailed him out. They put up 200 pounds, which was a great deal of money in those days. He was supposed to appear in January for trial, but his friends told him to run instead. When it was safe to come back, he went to court and got the large fine returned to them. He was discharged by proclamation.

Sarah Wilds, the wife of John Wilds from Topsfield, went through the normal accusations with her firm denials. The result was, as always that she was held over for trial.

Edward and Sarah Bishop, of Topsfield, were both tried that day, with the usual result. Edward was the stepson of Bridget Bishop. Sarah Bishop was the sister of John Wilds and possibly the niece of Rebecca Nurse. (Notice the interrelationships starting to surface.) At the time of their arrest, Edward and Sarah had twelve children. Luckily they were able to escape from prison, sparing them from the torment most of the other accused would soon be faced with.

Nehemiah Abbot, also from Topsfield, was an older man with a very authoritative voice. When he spoke some of the afflicted girls lost their composure. When the magistrates asked them if he hurt them, they came out with a split decision. Mary Walcott and Ann Putnam Junior claimed that he was the one, but Mercy Lewis said, "He is not the man!" Then, Mary Walcott started to waiver.

The magistrates suggested that Abbot step outside into the daylight, so that the girls could get a better look at him. The girls studied his pock-marked face at length. They all said that he was similar, but not the same as the man that tormented them. His voice must have upset them just enough to put a little fear into them. He was exonerated and sent home. He may not have gotten clear though. Mentioned later there was an arrest of a man named Abbot from the same area. No surname was given, but there weren't many people by that name living in the area.

Mary Black, a black slave of Nathaniel Putnam, was so ignorant that she didn't even understand why she was there or what a witch was. Her main answer to the questions put to her was, "I don't know." She was sent to prison, where she remained until May of 1693, when the governor released her by proclamation.

Mary English was the wife of one of the biggest merchants in Salem. When the marshal came to her house to arrest her, he was shown to her bed chamber. He read the arrest warrant to her; then he posted guards around the house for the night.

The next morning, Mary held a religious service with her family, very calmly kissed her children, spoke of the way she felt they should be educated, and told the marshal she was ready to die. She was under the rightful impression that an accusation from the afflicted children meant certain death. She was processed in the usual way and sent to await trial.

Mary Easty, the wife of Isaac Easty of Topsfield, was the most significant person tried that day. Two of her sisters, Rebecca Nurse and Sarah Cloyse, were already facing trial. The mother of seven, she was about 57 years old.

Her hearing started with the children's torments, followed by Hathorne's questions. When he asked how she could deny her guilt when it was apparent to all that she hurt the children, she replied, "Would you have me accuse myself?"

"How far have you gone with Satan?"

"Sir! I have never gone with him! I have prayed against him, always. What do you want me to do?"

"Confess, if you're guilty."

"I will say it one more time; I am not guilty of this sin!"

Hathorne wavered because of her forceful answer. Uncertain of her guilt he asked the girls, "Are you certain of this woman?"

All the girls had great fits. Then Ann Putnam Junior said, "That was the woman; it was just like her; she told me her name."

Mary Easty clasped her hands together and Mercy Lewis's hands locked together. When Mary unclasped her hands Mercy's did also. Mary Easty tilted her head and the girls screamed, "Straighten out her head, or our necks will be broken!"

Hathorne asked again, "Is this the woman?"

The girls acted as if they couldn't speak. Finally some of them cried out, "Oh, Goody Easty, Goody Easty, you are the woman, you are the woman!"

"What do you say to this?" asked Hathorne.

"Why? God will know."

"No, God knows now."

"I know he does!" she said.

"What did you think about all this before your sisters were accused? Did you think it was witchcraft?"

"I can't tell you."

"Why, don't you think it's witchcraft?"

"It's an evil spirit, but whether it's witchcraft, I do not know!"

She was, of course, committed to prison with the others.

The prosecutors became upset with the way the magistrates had handled this hearing. They had allowed Abbot to go free and they wavered on Mary Easty's guilt. This was not acceptable. The rigid methods used in the past would have to be adhered to if the hearings were to bear any weight.

They wrote the magistrates a letter, hinting in it that a conspiracy was behind all these witches and soon they would have the full gravity of it revealed to them. To put it in their words, "... thought it our duty to inform Your Honors of what we think you have not heard, which are very dreadful, about a wheel within a wheel, at which our ears tingle." Thomas Putnam's signature closed out the letter.

On the 30th of April, Jonathan Walcott and Thomas Putnam swore out warrants on Phillip English, the husband of Mary, on Sarah Morrel, and on Dorcas Hoar. Sarah and Dorcas were arrested May 2, but Phillip was nowhere to be found.

Sarah Morrel was found guilty and sent to prison for trial. A lack of trial records indicates that she survived the gallows and suffered a long waiting period in prison until amnesty was finally declared.

Dorcas Hoar's appearance in the meeting room caused the usual commotion with the afflicted girls, as they threw accusations at her. Hathorne asked, "Why do you hurt these girls?"

"I never hurt a child in my whole life!"

The girls charged that she had killed her husband. Then Abigail Williams, Mary Walcott, and Susanna Sheldon (18) said that a man in black was whispering in her ear.

Dorcas lost her temper saying, "Oh, you are liars, and God will punish liars!"

The magistrates took offense to her remark. "You are not to speak like this in court!"

"I will speak the truth as long as I live!" she shot back at them.

She was of course sent to prison for trial.

Phillip English was a man of great wealth. Among his holdings were fourteen buildings in Salem, a wharf, and twenty-one merchant ships. Why he was accused isn't very clear. He was a complete stranger to the girls, although no one would have thought so at the hearing. It is believed that his dealings generated a lot of animosity and jealousy. Some of his land disputes had to do with land in Salem Village; this was probably the cause for the girls' accusation.

He managed to elude the police for several weeks. On May 6 a general warrant was issued in Boston. He was eventually arrested, and on May 31 he was taken before the magistrates and condemned to trial.

Phillip English was put in the same cell as his wife, Mary. Reunited, they escaped to New York, where they remained as guests of the governor until the insanity was over. When the time came, they returned to Salem and continued with their lucrative business.

On April 30, the Widow Susanna Martin of Amesbury was arrested. She was an exceedingly neat person, a bit short and a bit plump. Her will was strong with an obvious intelligence and an outspoken nature. She was very active and took no guff from anyone.

Her hearing took place on May 2.

Hathorne asked the children, "Has this woman hurt you?"

Abigail Williams said she'd hurt her several times. Ann Putnam Junior threw a glove at the accused, and the other girls acted as if they couldn't speak. Susanna started laughing.

"What! You laugh at them?"

"I sure do at such stupidity!"

"Is it stupid to see them hurt so?"

"I never hurt a man, woman, or child."

"She's hurt me many times and thrown me down!" said Mercy Lewis.

Susanna started laughing again.

"What do you say to this?" Asked Hathorne.

"I do not practice witchcraft!"

"What do you do? Do you agree that they should be hurt?"

"No, never in my entire life!"

"What hurts these people?"

"I don't know."

"But, what do you think hurts them?"

"I don't want to express my opinion on it."

"Do you think they are bewitched?"

"No, I don't think they are!"

"Well, tell us what are your thoughts on the subject?"

"My thoughts are mine alone when I have them inside myself. But if I bring them out, they are everybody's."

"Who do you think is their master?"

"If they dabble in the black arts, you know who it is as well as

I do."

"What have you done toward hurting them?"

"I have done nothing!"

"But it's your specter."

"I can't help that!"

"How come your specter hurts them now?"

"How should I know?"

"Aren't you willing to tell the truth?"

"I don't know. If the Devil can appear in the prophet Samuel's shape, he can appear in anybody's shape."

"Do you believe the afflicted are telling the truth?"

"They may be lying, for all I know!"

"Maybe you're lying?"

"I can't tell a lie, even if it would save my life!"

The marshal said that she clenched her hands together. Elizabeth Hubbard had a fit in response to it. Pandemonium broke out among the afflicted girls. The magistrates became angry at this display.

"Pray God discovers you, if you are guilty!'"

"Amen, amen. Lies will never make a person guilty."

The afflicted became worse in their cries of torment.

"Don't you have any compassion for these afflicted people?"

"No, I have none!"

The afflicted intensified their actions even further. Then one of them said she could see Satan standing by Susanna's side. They pretended to try to walk up to her but were not able to walk. John Indian started toward her and fell to the floor.

"What is the reason they can't come near you?"

"I don't know. Maybe the Devil holds a grudge against me!"

"Don't you see that it is God showing us what you are?"

"No, not at all!"

"Everybody else thinks so."

"Let them think what they will."

"What is the reason they can't come near you?"

"I think they could, if they wanted to, or else if you want, I will go to them."

"What was the man in black whispering to you?"

"There was no one whispering to me!"

Susanna Martin was sent to prison for trial.

George Burroughs was a humble servant of the Lord. He had served as minister to Salem Village before Samuel Parris. His self-sacrificing ministry had taken him down to the coast of Maine, where he worked with the frontier settlements. Mister Burroughs was a small man with a dark complexion. He lived a laborious life

53

trying to help the less fortunate. The frontier settlement of Wells became his home.

Thomas Putnam and the other prosecutors had hinted to the magistrates that a secret most hideous was about to be revealed. A plot by Putnam and others had been nurturing for quite a while. Several of the afflicted girls had mentioned a man in black or a black man. He was described as the leader in the Satanic rituals. If they could find such a man, he would cause a commotion of such vast magnitude that the people would believe anything that was put before them. George Burroughs was chosen to be that man. Carefully they laid out their plan.

Abigail Hobbs had put the idea into the prosecutors' heads when she told them of the scandals she'd heard about while living at Casco Bay. The afflicted girls had picked up on all of this and started combining these stories with their own.

On April 20, Ann Putnam Junior made some astonishing disclosures to her father in the presence of Peter Prescott, Robert Morrel, and Ezekiel Cheever. Her father, Thomas Putnam, took her deposition and had her sign it.

She claimed to have seen the specter of a minister. The minister tried to get her to sign the book, but she refused. Then she told him that she felt it was a shame that he, a man of God, should have sold his soul to the Devil.

She asked him his name and he told her it was George Burroughs. He went on to tell her that he had killed two of his three wives by bewitchment and that he had killed Reverend Lawson's wife because she didn't want to leave the village; and he killed Lawson's daughter because Lawson went to preach to the soldiers. She claimed that he said he had made Abigail Hobbs a witch and several others. He said he was above a witch; he was a conjurer.

The men swore to the fact that Ann had told them all of this. The next day Thomas Putnam wrote the letter to the magistrates, with the hints of something big about to happen.

On April 21, Abigail Williams told Benjamin Hutchinson that she had seen a man who looked like George Burroughs: "... a little black minister that lived in Casco Bay." She said he'd told her he'd killed three wives, two for himself and one for Reverend Lawson. Hutchinson asked her where she had seen Burroughs, to which she replied, "There he is!" pointing to a rut in the road. Hutchinson had a pitchfork which he hurled at the spot.

"You've hit him, I heard his coat tear!"

"Where did I hit him?"

"On one side."

They came to Ingersoll's house and went in. Abigail stepped in and said, "There he stands!"

"Where? Where?" as he drew his sword.

"He's gone, but there is a gray cat in his place."

"Where abouts?"

"There! There!"

He struck at the spot, and Abigail fell into a fit. When she came out of it she said that he had killed it. Mister Hutchinson hadn't seen anything when he struck, but believing her, he took her word for it.

The prosecutors made several depositions, describing Burroughs alleged crimes against the church. When they were certain of its outcome they put their plan to work.

If George Burroughs had heard of what was about to happen, he would have run into the wilderness, and no one would have been able to catch him.

To prevent anyone from finding out, the plotters went to Boston. On April 30, Elisha Hutchinson issued an arrest warrant which was taken directly to the field marshal of Maine and New Hampshire, John Partridge. He arrested Burroughs and delivered him to Salem Village on May 4.

Shortly before Burroughs arrest, the girls started naming him as the man in black. The timing had been just right to prevent any possibility of his being warned.

CHAPTER VI

THE MAN IN BLACK

May 3, 1692 - May 13, 1692

In order to generate as much public interest in the case as possible and create in the public's mind a great disliking for George Burroughs, Deliverance Hobbs was brought into the picture. As the reader will remember, she was the mother of the confessed witch, Abigail Hobbs. Her hearing had caused her to break down and claim that she also was a witch. She had accused several other people of practicing witchcraft. None of those named were new to the magistrates. On May 3, someone told her about the Reverend Burroughs' arrest. That same day she submitted a confession to the magistrates.

"The First Examination of Deliverance Hobbs in Prison: She continues to freely admit that she is a witch, and further confesses that she was told of a meeting yesterday morning, present at that meeting were Proctor and his wife, Goody Nurse, Giles Corey and his wife, Goody Bishop and Mister Burroughs who was their preacher. He asked them to bewitch all the people in the village, telling them that they shouldn't do it all at once, but gradually, assuring them that they would prevail. He administered the sacrament to them at the same time, with red bread and red wine like blood.

"She affirms that she saw Osborne, Sarah Good, and Goody Wilds. Goody Nurse and Goody Wilds distributed the bread and wine; and a man in a long, crowned, white hat sat next to the minister. And they sat seemingly at a table; and they filled tankards with wine. She was told of this meeting by Goody Wilds. She states that she didn't eat or drink, but all the others did; therefore, they tormented her.

"The meeting was in the pasture by Mister Parris's house, and she saw when Abigail ran out to speak with them. But, by the time

Abigail had gone a short distance from the house, Deliverance was struck blind, so that she couldn't see who Abigail Williams talked to.

"She further said that Goody Wilds, in order to get her to sign the book, promised her new clothes and wouldn't hurt her anymore. At that same time her daughter, Abigail Hobbs, was brought in and was immediately taken with a great fit. And Deliverance, upon being asked who it was who hurt her daughter said it was Giles Corey, and she saw him and the gentlewoman of Boston (Misses English) trying to break her daughter's neck."

This testimony was exactly what the magistrates had hoped for. It would clinch their case against the soon-to-be-delivered minister.

George Burroughs was sitting at the table eating his humble meal when the marshals walked in. They grabbed him and dragged him off without giving him time to finish his meal or make any arrangements for his family's welfare. No explanation was given to him or his family. He was brought to Salem jail on May 4.

As soon as his capture became known, arrangements were made to make a public spectacle of his hearing. William Stoughton from Dorchester and Samuel Sewall from Boston came down to Salem Village to join Hathorne and Corwin in the examination. This would give the proceedings more solemnity. William Stoughton would preside.

"The Deposition of Ann Putnam Junior, who testifies and says that, 'On the eighth of May, in the evening, I saw the specter of Mister George Burroughs, who grievously tortured me, and urged me to write in his book, which I refused. He then told me that his first two wives would soon appear to me, and tell me a great many lies, but I should not believe them.

'Then immediately appeared to me the forms of two women dressed in sheets with napkins on top of their heads, at which I was greatly afraid. And they turned their faces toward Mister Burroughs, very red and angry, and told him that he had been very cruel to them, and that their blood cried for vengeance against him. And also told him that they should be clothed in white robes in heaven, and he should be thrown into hell, and immediately he vanished.

'And as soon as he was gone, the two women turned toward me, and looked as pale as a white wall, and told me that they were Mister Burroughs's first two wives, and that he had murdered them. And one of them told me that she was his first wife, and he stabbed her under her left arm, and put a piece of sealing wax in the wound. And she pulled aside her sheet and showed me her wound, and also told me that she was in the house of Mister Parris, when it was done.

'And the other woman told me that Mister Burroughs and his present wife killed her in the carriage as she was coming to visit her friends, because they wanted to be together. And the two women asked that I should tell these things to the magistrates in front of Mister Burroughs, and if he did not admit to them, they thought they might appear there.

'This morning Misses Lawson and her daughter Ann appeared to me, whom I knew, and told me that Mister Burroughs murdered them. This morning also appeared another woman in a sheet, and told me that she was Mister Fuller's first wife, and Mister Burroughs killed her, because there was some disagreement between him and her husband.'"

This deposition was given in front of her father, Thomas, and her Uncle Edward. It was considered by most people to be too descriptive for a girl of her tender years, and as such, must have been the truth. It didn't enter anyone's mind that this was a preposterous lie. With hindsight, it can be said that she was an abnormally well-informed little girl, with a persuasive gift of gab. Her testimony in all the trials to come would be the fatal blow to the accused.

On May 9, a special session of the Magistrate was held. First, a private hearing involving just the magistrates and ministers was conducted. At this hearing, George Burroughs was indicted on his differences in doctrine from that of the other ministers. None of this had to do with witchcraft. He was accused of missing communion services on one or two occasions and that only his oldest child had been baptized. Whether or not these two charges were true isn't known, but neither is proof of witchcraft. The secret inquisition lasted but a short while. At its conclusion, he was taken to the meetinghouse for a public hearing.

The turmoil from the afflicted girls greeted him as he came in. When it had subsided, Susanna Sheldon said, "His two wives appeared to me dressed in sheets and said that he'd killed them."

The magistrate ordered him to look at his accuser. As he did this, most of the afflicted fell to the ground as if pushed down. The afflicted children repeated their accusations while going in and out of their fits. Several of them had such disturbing fits that they were ordered removed from the room. Their suffering had become too hideous to watch. George Burroughs was asked what he thought of all of this.

"It was an amazing and humbling display of divine providence, but I know nothing about it."

Mister Burroughs was accused of lifting a rifle by stuffing a finger in its barrel. This amazing show of strength, for such a small man, was conceived as only being possible if he was in league with the Devil. There were several statements regarding his unusual feats of strength. While he attended Cambridge he had become a body builder, and became recognized as a skilled gymnast. Things that were easy for him to accomplish seemed impossible to those untrained, and they felt he couldn't do them without the Devil's help.

The afflicted were brought back into the room and the hearing continued. Abigail Hobbs, the confessed witch, said that she had seen Mister Burroughs in the field next to Mister Parris's house, conducting a witch's meeting. This backed up her mother's testimony. Mary Warren said Burroughs had a trumpet, which he blew to assemble the witches for their feasts. The trumpet carried a long distance and was only able to be heard by the confederates of Satan in the area. Interwoven with this testimony were the pretenses of the girls to choke. They would lose consciousness, then awaken, accusing Mister Burroughs or one of the other people already accused. They were careful not to mention any new names so as not to distract the audience from Mister Burroughs.

George Burroughs was handed over for trial.

On May 10, Sarah Osborne died in prison. Her ill health, combined with her age and prison conditions, had been too much of a strain. On that same day, warrants were served on George Jacobs Senior and his granddaughter, Margaret, both of Salem.

Thomas Beadle's house and Nathaniel Ingersoll's house were both inns with taverns on the ground floor. The meetinghouse, also known as the church, was around the corner from Ingersoll's. The two prisoners were taken to Thomas Beadle's house for this particular hearing. George Jacobs Senior was the first to be brought before the magistrates.

"Here are the people that accuse you of witchcraft."

Abigail Williams was the first to speak and put on her act. George couldn't help but laugh at her antics. He explained, "I laugh because I'm falsely accused. Your Worships, do you believe I'm speaking the truth?"

"No, what do you think?"

"I never did it."

"Who did it?"

"Don't ask me!"

"Why shouldn't we ask you? Sarah Churchill accuses you and there she is."

"I'm as innocent as a newborn child. I have lived for 33 years in Salem."

"What could it be then?"

"If you could prove that I'm guilty, I would confess to it."

"Sarah Churchill said, "Last night I was afflicted at Mister Ingersoll's."

Mary Walcott said, "It was a man with two canes. It was you, my master!"

"Pray do not accuse me. I'm as innocent as your worships, you must judge me properly."

"What book did he bring you, Sarah?"

"The same one the other woman brought."

"The Devil can come in any shape," said George.

"Didn't he appear on the other side of the river and hurt you?" asked Hathorne.

"Yes, he did," said Sarah.

"Look there, she accuses you to your face; she charges you with hurting her twice. Is it not true?"

"What would you have me say? I have not harmed anyone in word nor deed!"

"Here are three people giving evidence against you."

"You accuse me of being a wizard; you may as well charge me with being a buzzard. I have done no harm."

"Isn't it harmful to hurt these children?"

"I never did it!"

"But how come the specter looks like you?"

"The Devil can appear in any likeness."

"Not without the person's consent."

"Please, Your Worship, it's not true. I never showed the book. I am as ignorant about these things as a newborn child."

"That's what you say. You argue that you have lived too long, but how long had Cain lived before he killed Abel, and you might have lived a long time before you made a bargain with the Devil."

"Christ suffered three times for me."

"He suffered the Cross and gall--"

Sarah Churchill interrupted him, "You had it good, confess if you are guilty."

"Have you heard of me using any witchcraft?"

"I know you've led a wicked life," she said.

"Let her prove it."

"Does he ever pray to his family?" asked Hathorne.

"Not unless he's by himself," she said.

"Why do you not pray to your family?"

"I cannot read."

"Well, you should still be able to pray. Can you say the Lord's

Prayer? Let's hear you?"

The poor old man tried several times to say it right, but each time he stumbled. His memory had failed him in this most critical of moments.

"Sarah Churchill, when you wrote in the book you said you were shown your master's name."

"Yes, sir!"

"If she says so, how do you know it's true?" George asked the magistrate.

"But she saw you, or your likeness trying to make her write."

"Someone else in my likeness; the Devil can make my likeness!"

"Were you not frightened, Sarah Churchill, when the specter of your master came to you?"

"Yes!"

"Well, you can burn me or hang me. I stand in the truth of Christ. I know nothing about it!"

"Do you know nothing about getting your son, George, or his daughter, Margaret, to sign?"

"No, nothing at all!"

He was taken to jail without a decision being reached. The magistrates felt that he might be telling the truth and wanted to hear more of his testimony. The next morning, May 11, he was brought back in. The afflicted girls showed up in force, determined to put him away. They broke into great fits as soon as he walked into the room.

"Is this the man that hurts you?"

Abigail Williams screamed, "That's the man," and had a violent fit. Ann Putnam said, "That's the man. He's hurting me and he's bringing me the book to sign and telling me I'll be just as well as his granddaughter if I sign it."

"Mercy Lewis, is this the man?"

"This is the man." She had several fits. "He hurts me."

Elizabeth Hubbard said he hadn't hurt her until that day.

"Mary Walcott, is this the man?"

Several fits broke out, then she answered, "This is the man; he used to come with two canes and beat me."

"Do you still say you're not a witch?"

"No, I am not, even if it means my life!"

Mercy Lewis tried to walk up to him, but fell down in a fit.

"What do you say to this?"

"Why, it's a lie. I know nothing about it, anymore than an unborn child would know."

Ann Putnam said, "Yes, you do. You told me you've been doing it for forty years."

Ann Putnam and Abigail Williams showed the magistrates their hands. There were pins sticking in them. They both accused the old man of having put them there.

Abigail Williams testimony was read. When it was finished, the magistrate asked George, "Aren't you the man that made a disturbance at a Lecture in Salem?"

"It wasn't a great disturbance. Do you think I used witchcraft?"

"Yes, indeed!"

"No, I used none!"

George Jacobs Senior was sent to prison to await trial.

In the county clerk's office, an interesting piece of evidence was discovered that was never used. It was a deposition given by Sarah Ingersoll and witnessed by Ann Andrews, George Jacobs Senior's daughter.

"The Deposition of Sarah Ingersoll, aged about thirty years. Saying that Sarah Churchill, after her examination, came to me crying and wringing her hands, seeming to be very troubled. I asked her what was troubling her. She answered, saying that she'd done something wrong. I asked her what. She said she lied to herself and the others by saying she'd signed the Devil's book. She claimed she never had.

"I told her I believed she'd signed it. She answered, crying, 'No! No! I never, I never did!' I asked her what made her say she did. She answered, because the others threatened her, and told her they would put her into the dungeon with Mister Burroughs; and she followed me back and forth and told me she'd really done wrong telling lies to everybody.

"I asked her why she didn't deny she wrote in the book. She told me she's been mixed up in this thing so long that she dared not. She also said that if she told Mister Noyes she wrote in the book only once, he would believe her; but if she told him a hundred times that she hadn't, he wouldn't believe her."

Sarah Ingersoll was married to the son of Nathaniel Ingersoll's brother. A widow, in later years she would become the second wife of the rich Salem merchant, Phillip English. The document was believed to have been written on the evening of George Jacobs first hearing.

It was obvious that Sarah Churchill felt remorse for having lied about her master. The other girls had threatened her with prison if she said anything to discredit them at the hearing the next morning. There is no mention of her being at the second hearing. It is also interesting to note that the girls knew Mister

Burroughs had been put in a dungeon, even though he hadn't been brought to trial yet. This document was the closest thing to a confession ever made during the witch trials.

The papers of Margaret Jacobs's hearing were lost. There will be more about her later, but at this point she had been committed to prison to await trial.

On May 10, the same day as the Jacobs's hearings, a warrant was issued for the arrest of deputy constable, John Willard. Constable John Putnam Junior searched for him, but could not find him. Willard's relatives believed he had fled. On May 15, a general warrant was issued throughout New England. He was apprehended in Groton and delivered to Thomas Beadle's house on May 18.

John Willard's story is of great interest. He had the job of bringing in the accused persons. The shabby treatment and heavy shackling of the prisoners disturbed him. The things he heard and saw made him sympathetic toward them. He voiced his opinions to others. Once while visiting a relative, he was heard to say that all the people involved in the prosecution of these people should be hung, as they were all witches.

John Willard was the grandson of Bray Wilkins. Bray and most of his neighbors disliked John. When rumors started spreading about John's being in league with the Devil, John became disturbed and went to his grandfather for help. His grandfather told him he couldn't help him, because he was going on a trip and wouldn't be home until dark.

Willard was to travel to Boston with Bray's son, Henry, at election time; but Henry's son, Daniel, disapproved of his father's associating with Willard and tried to talk him out of it. Henry's son felt that Willard should be hanged.

Bray Wilkins and his wife also went to Boston for the elections. The old couple made the trip on horseback. They had a grand time, and on election day they went to Dorchester to dine with Bray's brother. While Bray was there, Willard arrived. John Willard hadn't liked the way his grandfather had shunned him when he needed his help. Bray thought he saw Willard giving him a contemptuous look. Immediately afterwards, the many parties and general excitement took their toll on the old man. Bray suffered a heart attack. He told his wife that he thought the pain was brought on by Willard. A woman skilled in medicine looked him over and said she thought he was being afflicted.

On his way home, Bray found out that his grandson, Daniel, the same one that had warned Henry Wilkins about Willard, was in great pain and dying. Bray suffered another heart attack.

The people in Will's Hill were disturbed by all of this suffering. Mister Parris brought in Mercy Lewis and Mary Walcott to see if they could find out who was afflicting Bray and his grandson.

It didn't take them long to claim that they saw old Misses Buckley and John Willard at Daniel's throat, choking him and pressing on his chest.

When Mercy Lewis walked into Bray's room, she pretended to look around. The people in the room asked her whether she was looking for something. "Yes, I am looking for John Willard." Then she said, "There he is on his grandfather's belly!" Later the old man said in his deposition that his belly hurt a great deal at that instant.

Ann Putnam Senior made a deposition at this same time accusing John Willard of several murders. Several other people made depositions against Willard. His hearing was held on May 18 and he was committed for trial.

On the 12th of May, warrants were issued for Ann Pudeator, a widow of Salem, and Alice Parker, wife of John Parker of Salem. They were taken to Thomas Beadle's for examination.

The Examination of Alice Parker:

"Mary Warren charges you with several acts of witchcraft. How do you plead, guilty or not guilty?"

"I am not guilty."

"You told her today that you got rid of Thomas Westgate."

"I know nothing about it."

"You told her John (Lapthons) was (lost) in (???)."

"I never spoke a word to her in my life!"

"You also told her that you bewitched her sister because her father wouldn't mow your grass."

"I never saw her before."

Mary Warren asked if she could go up and slap Alice. The magistrates said it was okay. Mary started toward Alice Parker, but fell to the floor in a dreadful fit before she could reach her.

Margaret Jacobs charged that she saw Alice's specter in the north field on Friday night at around nine o'clock.

Marshal Herrick said that she told him, after he had arrested her and was bringing her to be examined, that there were sixty witches of the company, which he didn't deny. He said she didn't remember how many she had said there were.

Mary Warren stated that her father had said he would cut the grass for Alice Parker if he had time, which he didn't, so she came to the house and told him he should have done it. A little while later her sister became ill, then her mother became ill and died.

Mary Warren stated that when Alice brought the doll to her,

she said if Mary didn't stick it with a pin, then Alice would stick it into her heart.

Mary confirmed it in front of Alice Parker. When Alice looked at her, Mary immediately fell into a fit.

When Alice was asked about these charges, she wished that God would open up the earth and swallow her if one word was true and make her an example for the others. At the same time as she said this, Mary Warren had a terrible fit.

Mary said that Alice told her this very morning that she was at the blood sacrament in Mister Parris's pasture, and (that) there were about thirty of them. She said that Alice told her that she ran after John Londer in the Common.

Mary claimed that Alice's specter tormented her throughout the hearing.

Mister Noyes said that when Alice Parker was sick he talked with her about her practicing witchcraft. He wanted to know if she was guilty. She answered that if she was as free from other sins as she was of witchcraft, she wouldn't have to ask for the Lord's mercy. Mary Warren had a terrible fit at this time. Her tongue was black. Alice said Mary's tongue would be a lot blacker before she died.

Alice was asked why she afflicted Mary so. She answered, "If I do, the Lord forgive me!"

The above testimony was probably written by Samuel Parris. Name repetition was cut down for ease of reading. Parris took superficial notes that missed a lot of other testimony.

[Authors note: There was another Parker (Mary) arrested in September with very similar background to Alice. Because of this, their records were mixed up. A careful study of the dates and the surrounding testimony indicates the following testimony belongs to Alice Parker.]

The most damaging piece of testimony came from John Westgate. John Westgate was in Beadle's Tavern with several friends, including Alice's husband, John. Alice didn't approve of her husband's drinking, and the people with whom he drank. She came storming into the place and scolded him, saying that he was a good for nothing. Westgate took her husband's side, saying Alice was behaving unladylike - coming into a tavern after her husband. Alice turned on him, calling him a rogue and told him to mind his own business. She went on to tell him he shouldn't say anything.

Several drinks later, Westgate walked home with his dog by his side. What happened next is his version of the story. As he walked down the street, a big black hog came charging out at him. It looked like it would eat him in one gulp. Turning to run, he tripped and fell, driving his knife into his hip, all the way up to the hilt.

When he got up, his shoe and sock were full of blood. He was forced to crawl along the fence all the way home. The hog followed him all the way home. His large dog, a known hog killer, ran off whining as soon as Westgate fell. When he arrived home, Westgate found his knife still in its sheath. He pulled his knife out and the sheath fell apart. The hog must have been a devil sent by Alice Parker to torment him.

What really happened that night was a case of too much drink. He left the tavern with his dog at his side. Somewhere along the road he tripped and fell in a drunken stupor. As he rolled forward he landed on his knife, breaking the sheath. The blade probably cut his skin. Like most drunks, his voice was probably very loud as he fell, thus frightening the dog. His drunken imagination did the rest. The hog following him home could have been the dog coming back from his scared flight. Why his dog didn't see the hog and come to his defense is easily explained. He was drunk, the dog was not.

The magistrates accepted his warped version of the story. It suited their purposes better than the truth.

Ann Pudeator was brought in front of the magistrates on May 12. An old woman in her 70s, the charges were deemed too vague to convict her and she was released. On July 2, she was brought before the court again and held over for trial.

CHAPTER VII

OYER AND TERMINER

May 14, 1692 - May 31, 1692

After months at sea, Increase Mather arrived in Massachusetts with the new charter. Increase had used his influence on King William and Queen Mary to have Sir William Phips installed as the new governor. With the help of Cotton Mather, Increase Mather's son, William Stoughton, replaced Thomas Danforth as deputy governor. The Council which had consisted of John Hathorne, Jonathan Corwin, Samuel Appleton, and Robert Pike had a new member. His name was Bartholomew Gedney.

The new government felt it best not to interfere with the witch hearings. Gedney was placed in charge of the magistrates. The number of indictments overwhelmed Governor Phips. He felt that the situation should be handled by those already close to it.

The council decided to appoint a special court of Oyer and Terminer (hear and determine). This court was an archaic form of an old English judicial system. Some people felt that creating this court without the vote of the people was illegal, as it shouldn't have the power to handle anything but civil cases. Stoughton was placed in charge. Saltonstall, Richards, Gedney, Sewall, Winthrop and Sargent were made associate judges.

On the same day, May 14, warrants were issued for Salem Village residents Daniel Andrew, George Jacobs Junior and his wife, Rebecca, and Sarah Buckley and her daughter, Mary Witheridge. Warrants were also issued for Thomas Farrer and Elizabeth Hart of Lynn, Elizabeth Colson of Reading, and Bethia Carter of Woburn.

Elizabeth Hart, Elizabeth Colson and Bethia Carter had nothing extraordinary happen at their hearings. They were examined and committed to Boston Jail to await trial. Several months later they were given amnesty.

Thomas Farrer was accused because his nose was larger than normal. Physical imperfection was one of the things the girls seemed to pick up on, probably because the person was easier to remember. George Jacobs Senior had been exceptionally tall and, with his two walking canes, must have stuck in their minds.

Daniel Andrew was one of the village leaders. When word came to him of his impending arrest, he and his good friend, George Jacobs Junior, escaped, taking up residence in a foreign country until the trials were over.

George Jacobs Junior's wife, Rebecca, was slightly insane but harmless. Her mental condition was well-known by the people around her and they were sympathetic to her. Margaret, her daughter, had been arrested. George had escaped and his father was in prison. These things pushed her fragile mind into even greater turmoil.

When the constable came to arrest her, she didn't want to go. He convinced her that she would only be gone for a short while. She had four small children. Those that were able to walk, followed her for quite a distance, trying to keep up with her. They were left alone in the middle of nowhere with no one to take care of them. Some of Rebecca's neighbors felt pity for the children and took them into their own homes to live.

Rebecca's imprisonment was an outrage to many people. Six months later, her mother petitioned the reigning governor, Sir William Phips. This sad plea is worthy of reading as it gives great insight into what these poor people went through. I have transcribed it below. Aside from some spelling corrections, I have left it in its original Old-English format.

"The Humble Petition of Rebecca Fox of Cambridge."

"Showeth that whereas Rebecca Jacobs (daughter of your humble petitioner) has a long time, even many months now lyen in prison for witchcraft & is well known to be a person craz'd distracted & broken in mind, your humble petitioner does most humbly & earnestly seek unto Your Excellency & to Your Hon'rs for relief in this case:

"Your petitioner who knows well the condition of her poor daughter, together with several others of good repute and credit are ready to offer their oaths that the s'd Jacobs is a woman craz'd distracted and broken of mind & that she has been so these twelve years & upwards;

"However for (I think) about this half year the s'd Jacobs has lyen in prison & yet remains there attended with many sore difficulties;

"Christianity & nature do each of them oblige your petitioner to be very solicitous in this matter, and although many weighty cases do exercise your thoughts, yet your humble petitioner can have no rest in her mind, till such time as she has offered this her address on behalf of her daughter:

"Some have dyed already in prison, and others have been dangerously sick, & how soon others, & among them my poor child, by the difficulties of this confinement may be sick and dye, G'd only knows:

"She is uncapable of making that shift for her self that others can do, & such are her circumstances on other accounts that your petitioner who is her tender mother has many great sorrows & almost overcoming burdens on her mind upon her account, but in the midst of all her perplexities and troubles (next to supplicating to a good & merciful God) your petitioner has no way for help but to make this her afflicted condition known unto you, so not doubting but Your Excellency and Your Hon'rs will readily hear the cries & groans of a poor distressed woman and grant what help and enlargement you may your petitioner heartily begs God's gracious presence with you and subscribes her self in all humble manner."

"Your sorrowful and distressed petitioner, Rebecca Fox"

As sad as this petition was, it went unanswered. On January 3, 1693, the grand jury found Rebecca Jacobs' indictment and acquitted her.

On May 18, Mary Easty, Rebecca Nurse's sister, was released from prison. The afflicted girls had become uncertain about whether they had seen her specter. Only Mercy Lewis clung to her story. As soon as Mary Easty was released from prison Mercy Lewis came down with violent convulsions. The people that saw her, felt that she didn't have long to live. It was suggested that Ann Putnam, Mary Warren, and Susanna Sheldon be brought over, to see if they could find out what was afflicting Mercy. The girls ran over and looked at Mercy's contorted form.

Without hesitation they said that they could see Mary Easty, choking Mercy Lewis. After a considerable amount of time had elapsed, Mercy came out of her fit and accused Mary Easty of trying to kill her. She claimed that it was the only way that Mary could stop her from being the only witness against her. A warrant was issued for Mary's arrest. She was arrested and returned to prison on May 20.

The hearings for Sarah Buckley and her daughter, Mary Witheridge, were held at Ingersoll's house, on May 18.

The only surviving record of Mary Witheridge's hearing was a deposition by Elizabeth Hubbard. It contained very weak claims that Mary had afflicted her and three of the other girls on the day of her hearing. Sadly, the magistrates accepted even weak evidence such as this and she was committed to prison.

Sarah Buckley's hearing opened with the afflicted girls putting on their usual display. As each girl was carried to Sarah, she was made to touch her. Immediately the girl would cease her fit and walk back to her place in a normal fashion. The magistrates committed her to prison for trial.

Sarah Buckley was a very poor woman, but was well-liked by the clergy. At the request of her husband, William Buckley, three of them boldly offered documents in her defense. These documents were written at a time when fear kept most people from saying anything against the hearings. For that reason they are of great significance:

"This is to certify to whom it may concern that I have known Sarah, wife of William Buckley of Salem Village, more or less, ever since she came from England, which is more than fifty years ago; and during all that time, I never knew or heard of her doing any evil, or conversation unbefitting a Christian. Likewise, she was brought up by Christian parents all the time she lived in Ipswich.

"I further testify that said Sarah was admitted as a member into the church of Ipswich about forty years ago; and that I never heard from others, or observed myself, anything that was inconsistent with her profession or unsuitable with Christianity, either with word, deed or conversation, and am strangely surprised that any person should speak or think of her as someone to be suspected of the crime she has been charged with. In testimony hereof I have set my hand this twentieth day of June, 1692, William Hubbard."

"Being desired by William Buckley to give my testimony to his wife's conversation before this great calamity befell her, I cannot refuse to bear witness to the truth; viz. that, during the time that she lived in Salem in communion with this church, having frequently conversed with her, I have never observed for myself, or heard from others, anything that was unsuitable in talking about the Gospel, and have always looked upon her as a Godly woman. Signed, John Higginson."

"Marblehead, January 2, 1693: Upon the same request, having had the opportunity by her residence at Marblehead, I can do no less than give her like testimony for her pious conversation during her abode in this place and communion with us. Signed, Samuel Cheever."

The first one was presented after the executions had started. The minister had good reason to believe his life would be in danger, but his conscience overrode his apprehension. The latter two were submitted near the end of the trials, but still took a lot of courage to write.

William Hubbard was a modest minister of the highest caliber. He was minister to Ipswich. He is remembered for his honor and devotion to the church. In later years he became known for his historical accounts of New England and of the French and Indian Wars.

John Higginson was pastor of the First Church of Salem. He wrote his document at the age of 76. Although he believed that witches existed, he didn't believe that these cases were legitimate. His outspokenness against the trials didn't miss the afflicted girls ears. They accused his daughter, Anna, the wife of Captain William Dolliver of Gloucester. She was arrested and sent to prison. None of this changed Higginson's opinions. He was given the well-deserved title of " Nestor of the New England Clergy."

Samuel Cheever was another of New England's most respected ministers, held in the highest regard by all that knew him.

Sarah Buckley and her daughter, Mary Witheridge, spent many months in prison, heavily chained and shackled. When they were acquitted in January of 1693, they had to remain in prison. Before they could get out, they had to pay the cost of their imprisonment, which consisted of their food, chains, arrest costs and court costs. The sum amounted to five pounds.

When this sum was finally paid, they were released into total poverty. Their meager property had been seized long ago by Sheriff George Corwin. Sheriff Corwin was the son-in-law of Judge Bartholomew Gedney, the nephew of Judge Jonathan Corwin and Judge Wait Still Winthrop.

Sheriff Corwin seems to have had a mercenary interest in the trials. If he arrested someone, their civil rights were taken from them. He would grab outlandish amounts of the accused person's property to collect the charges due the court. From the records that survive, it would be very easy to conclude that he was a profiteer on other people's misery. Several of the victims sued his estate for their losses. The following is an excerpt from an accounting submitted by Phillip English for reimbursement. For the reader's reference, a jailer received 20 pounds per year and a good cow sold for 2 pounds.

The first part of the document listed extensive goods taken from seven locations owned by Mister English. The total taken was 1,183 pounds and 2 shillings.

The document went on to state: "The foregoing is a true account of what I had seized, taken away, lost and embezzled while I was a prisoner in the year 1693, and while I was running for my life, besides a considerable quantity of household goods and other things, which I cannot give an exact accounting of. All I ever received for these claims was 60 pounds 3 shillings paid me by the administrators of the late Sheriff George Corwin's estate. My estate was seized and taken away chiefly by the sheriff and his under-officers. Besides all of this, I placed a surety bond of 4,000 pounds at Salem. Signed, Phillip English."

From May 21 onward, several warrants were issued for people living throughout the province of Massachusetts. Among these were three of John and Elizabeth Proctor's children, Benjamin, Sarah and William. The disease had gone out of control; no one was safe from the malicious lies of the afflicted children. I will touch on some of the more significant cases.

Martha Carrier was the mother of four children. At the time of her arrest, the children were also brought in. It had become common practice to persuade near relatives to make statements against the accused. Whatever was done to Martha's children turned them into her accusers. Her children gave fatal testimony against her. By the time Martha came in for her hearing, the children had been primed to tell a well-knit story. Cotton Mather, the son of Increase Mather, sat in on the hearing. A zealous witch hunter, he wanted nothing less than to see them brought to justice.

After her children and the afflicted girls made their accusations, the magistrates asked her questions.

"What do you say to these charges?"

"I haven't done it."

One of her accusers said that she was sticking pins in her; another said that Martha was talking to a black man.

"What black man is it?"

"I don't know any!" answered Martha.

"What black man did you see?"

"I saw no black man, only you standing here."

"Can you look at these children without knocking them down?"

"They will act crazy if I look at them!" The children fell to the ground.

"You see, you look at them and they fall down."

"It's not true; the Devil's a liar. I've looked at no one besides you, since I came in."

Susanna Sheldon cried out, "I wonder what you could murder thirteen persons for."

Martha Carrier became very angry. The accusers broke into awful fits. She accused the magistrate of being unfair, of taking their word for everything, and of accepting nothing she said. "It's a shameful thing that you should listen to these folks that are out of their minds!" She looked right at her accusers and said, "You lie! I have been wronged!" Her gutsy character threw the whole place into an uproar.

Parris summed up the uproar with these words: "The tortures of the afflicted were so great that there was no enduring it. She was ordered taken away, and tied hand and foot as quickly as possible. In the meanwhile, the afflicted had almost died in front of the spectators, magistrates and others."

Parris added a footnote to his report: "Note: As soon as she was well-bound, the afflicted became normal. Mary Walcott told the magistrates that Martha had told her she'd been a witch for forty years."

Like the many before her, Martha Carrier was committed to trial.

Elizabeth Cary was brought to the hearing by her husband, Jonathan, on May 24. Since rumor had it that his wife was being accused, he had wanted to know how the hearings were conducted. Most people of the period spelled phonetically, at best, and were almost illiterate. A ship's master, Jonathan Cary had an unusually fine writing style. He recorded the event from start to finish, together with his personal feelings. It is presented here, verbatim. *1692*

"May twenty-fourth. I having heard, some days that my wife was accused of witchcraft; being much disturbed at it, by advice went to Salem Village, to see if the afflicted knew her; we arrived on the twenty-fourth of May. It happened to be a day appointed for examination; accordingly, soon after our arrival, Mister Hathorne and Mister Corwin, &c., went to the meetinghouse, which was the place appointed for that work. The minister began with a prayer; I observed that the afflicted were two girls of about ten years old, and about two or three others of about eighteen; one of the girls talked most, and could discern more than the rest.

"The prisoners were called in one by one, and, as they came in, were cried out at, &c. The prisoners were placed about seven or eight feet from the justices, and the accusers between the justices and them. The prisoners were ordered to stand right before the justices, with an officer appointed to hold each hand, least they therewith afflict them; and the prisoners' eyes must be constantly on the justices; for if they looked on the afflicted, they would either fall into fits, or cry out of being hurt by them. After an examination of the prisoners, who it was afflicted these girls, &c., they were put upon saying the Lord's Prayer, as a trial of their guilt.

"After the afflicted seemed to be out of their fits, they would look steadfastly on some one person, and frequently not speak; and then the justices said that they were struck dumb, and after a little time would speak again: Then the justices said to the accusers, 'Which of you will go and touch the prisoner at the bar?' Then the most courageous would adventure, but, before they had made three steps, would ordinarily fall down as in a fit: The justices ordered that they should be taken up and carried to the prisoner that she might touch them; and as soon as they were touched by the accused, the justices would say, 'They are well,' before I could discern any alteration, -by which I observed that the justices understood the manner of it.

"Thus far I was only a spectator: My wife also was there part of the time, but no notice was taken of her by the afflicted, except once or twice they came to her, and asked her name. But I having an opportunity to discourse Mister Hale (with whom I had formerly acquaintance), I took his advise what I had best do, and desired of him that I might have an opportunity to speak with her that accused my wife; which he promised should be, I acquainted him that I reposed my trust in him.

"Accordingly, he came to me after the examination was over, and told me I had now an opportunity to speak with said accuser, Abigail Williams, a girl eleven or twelve years old; but that we could not be in private at Mister Parris's house, as he had promised me: We went therefore into the alehouse, where an Indian man attended us, who, it seems, was one of the afflicted; to him we gave some cider: He showed several scars that seemed as if they had been long there, and showed them as done by witchcraft, and acquainted us that his wife, who also was a slave, was imprisoned for witchcraft.

"And now, instead of one accuser, they all came in, and began to tumble like swine; and then three women were called in to attend them. We in the room were all at a stand to see who they would cry out of; but in a short time they cried out 'Cary:' And immediately after, a warrant was sent from the justices to bring my wife before them, who were sitting in a chamber near by, waiting for this.

"Being brought before the justices, her chief accusers were two girls. My wife declared to the justices that she never had any knowledge of them before that day. She was forced to stand with her arms stretched out. I requested that I might hold one of her hands, but it was denied me: Then she desired me to wipe the tears from her eyes, and the sweat from her face, which I did; then she desired she might lean herself on me, saying she should faint.

Justice Hathorne replied she had strength enough to torment these persons, and she should have strength enough to stand.

"I speaking something against their cruel proceedings, they commanded me to be silent, or else I should be turned out of the room. The Indian before mentioned was also brought in, to be one of her accusers; being come in, he now (when before the justices) fell down, and tumbled about like a hog, but said nothing. The justices asked the girls who afflicted the Indian: They answered she (meaning my wife), and that she now lay upon him.

"The justices ordered her to touch him, in order to his cure, but her head must be turned another way, lest, instead of curing, she should make him worse by her looking on him, her hand being guided to take hold of his; but the Indian took hold of her hand, and pulled her down on the floor in a barbarous manner: Then his hand was taken off, and her hand put on his, and the cure was quickly wrought.

"I being extremely troubled at their inhuman dealings, uttered a hasty speech, 'That God would take vengeance on them, and desired that God would deliver us out of the hands of unmerciful men.' Then her mittimus was writ.

"I did with difficulty and charge obtain the liberty of a room, but no beds in it; if there had been, could have taken but little rest that night. She was committed to Boston prison; but I obtained a habeas corpus to remove her to Cambridge prison, which is in our county of Middlesex. Having been there one night, next morning the jailer put irons on her legs (having received such a command); the weight of them was about eight pounds: These irons and her other afflictions soon brought her into convulsion fits, so that I thought she would have died that night. I sent to entreat that the irons might be taken off; but all entreaties were in vain, if it would have saved her live, so that in this condition she must continue.

"The trials at Salem coming on, I went thither to see how things were managed: And finding that the specter evidence was there received, together with idle, if not malicious stories, against people's lives, I did easily perceive which way the rest would go; for the same evidence that served for one would serve for all the rest. I acquainted her with her danger; and that, if she were carried to Salem to be tried, I feared she would never return.

"I did my utmost that she might have her trial in our own county; I with several others petitioning the judge for it, and were put in hopes of it: But I soon saw so much that I understood thereby it was not intended; which put me upon consulting the means of her escape, which, through the goodness of God, was effected, and she got to Rhode Island, but soon found herself not safe there, by reason of the pursuit after her; from thence she went to New York, along with some others that had escaped their cruel hands, where we found his Excellency Benjamin Fletcher, Esquire, Governor, who was very courteous to us.

"After this, some of my goods were seized in a friend's hands, with whom I had left them, and myself imprisoned by the sheriff, and kept in custody half a day, and then dismissed; but to speak of their usage of the prisoners, and the inhumanity shown to them at the time of their execution, no sober Christian could bear.

"They had also trials of cruel mockings, which is the more, considering what a people for religion, I mean the profession of it, we have been; those that suffered being many of them church members, and most of them unspotted in their conversation, till their adversary the Devil took up this method for accusing them."
Jonathan Cary

A family dispute between Perley and Howe brought on dire consequences. A heated discussion overheard by the ten-year-old daughter of Perley brought accusations against Elizabeth Howe. The child developed fits similar to the afflicted children. She claimed that Elizabeth had bewitched her. Within a short while every ache and pain felt by people in the area was blamed on Elizabeth. On the 31st of May, she was brought before the magistrates.

Elizabeth Howe was another woman held in high esteem by several of the populace. Many depositions were submitted in her defense. Two of the depositions were presented by Samuel Phillips and Reverend Payson, ministers of Rowley. Both men had gone to examine the Perley child. To test the child's honesty, they brought Elizabeth Howe along. Reverend Payson's deposition is presented here.

"Being in Perley's house for some considerable time before Misses Howe came in, their afflicted daughter, on something her mother said to her privately, presently fell into one of her strange fits, during which she made no mention (as I observed) of Misses Howe, or anything relating to her. Some time after, Misses Howe came in, when the girl's fit had ended. Said Howe took said girl by the hand, and asked her whether she had ever done her any harm. The child answered, 'No; never.' With several expressions of that meaning."

Samuel Phillips' testimony confirmed this event, with the addition of recording Samuel Perley's telling his sister, "Say Goodwife Howe is a witch; say she is a witch." Phillips commented, "No wonder that the child mentioned Howe in her fits when her nearest relatives frequently expressed their suspicions in the child's hearing as she comes out of her fits that Goodwife Howe is the cause of them."

Her father-in-law, James Howe Senior, told the court that, "I've lived by her for about 30 years. She has been a good woman, as a daughter-in-law, as a wife, in all relations, setting aside human differences, as becomes a Christian; with respect to myself as a father-in-law, very dutifully; and as a wife to my son, very careful, loving, obedient and kind, considering his lack of eyesight, tenderly leading him about by the hand. Desiring God may guide your honors, I rest, yours to serve."

In spite of all the testimony in her favor, Elizabeth Howe was sent to prison to await trial. Twice a week, her blind husband would make the long trip with one of their two daughters to visit her in prison. Her family loved her dearly and exhausted the little they had to be with her. One of the daughters made her way to Boston to beg the Governor for a reprieve, but the trip was in vain.

The reach of the afflicted children was constantly going out after the most respected and pious people. Mary Bradbury was another of these fine people. One hundred and seventeen people signed a document attesting to her goodness.

"Concerning Misses Bradbury's life and conversations, we, the signers, do testify that it was such as fits the Gospel: She was a lover of the ministry, in all things, and a diligent follower of God's holy ordinances, being courteous and peaceful in everything that she did. Neither did any of us (Some of whom have lived in town with her for over fifty years) ever heard or known that she ever had any difference or falling-out with any of her neighbors, man, woman or child. But, was always ready and willing to do for them whatever was in her power, day or night, through sickness or other danger. More could be spoken of her goodness, but this is enough for now."

Like Elizabeth Howe, the magistrates ignored the positive testimony and she was sent to prison. Later she was condemned to death. Her story ended happily; she escaped from prison and was spared the walk to the gallows.

CHAPTER VIII

THE TRIALS BEGIN

May 31, 1692 - June 8, 1692

Andover was a quiet community to the northwest of Salem Village. Reading lay to the southwest of Andover, and Topsfield lay to the east. One day, the wife of a very respectable man became sick. Her fever wouldn't subside and many people in the community began to think that she might be being tormented by someone evil. After much advice from his neighbors, the man went to Salem Village for help, a grave mistake.

He came back with those infallible witch hunters, Ann Putnam Junior and Abigail Williams. They were very quick to discover the persons responsible for his wife's affliction. Problems arose when they couldn't stop pointing the finger and naming names. Panic broke out among the townspeople. They felt that the only way not to be accused, would be to accuse someone else first, a feeling to be shared by many in the near future. By the time forty people had been arrested, the local magistrate, Dudley Bradstreet, son of the previous Governor, felt something was wrong with the whole thing. In good conscience he refused to sign any more arrest warrants.

The next thing Bradstreet knew, he and his wife had been accused. Bradstreet had no other choice: he and his wife fled. Not finding him the next accusation was aimed at his brother John. The accusers said that John had afflicted a dog. John Bradstreet also got away, but the dog wasn't so lucky. He was executed as being possessed. By the time the accusations were finished, over fifty people had been sent to prison and several more accusers had joined the ranks of the afflicted girls. The effect mushroomed to other communities, filling the local jails to overwhelming capacity. Several of the people from Andover would lose their lives in the months to follow.

Captain John Alden was brought before the magistrates on

May 31. He had the dubious honor of being "the tall man from Boston," the afflicted girls had talked about from the very beginning. Why he had been chosen remains a mystery. It is fairly certain that the girls had never met him. One guess is that his naval military position had made an enemy in Salem Village, and that enemy had made certain that the girls would pick up his name and description. He dictated his experiences to an acquaintance. For this we are eternally grateful, as it is the only first hand account (from an accused person) on record. It is presented here.

"An Account how John Alden, Senior, was dealt with at Salem Village."

"John Alden, Senior, of Boston, in the county of Suffolk, mariner, on the twenty-eighth day of May, 1692, was sent for by the magistrates of Salem, in the county of Essex, upon the accusation of a company of poor distracted or possessed creatures or witches; and, being sent by Mister Stoughton, arrived there on the thirty-first of May, and appeared at Salem Village before Mister Gedney, Mister Hathorne, and Mister Corwin.

"Those wenches being present who played their juggling tricks, falling down, crying out, and staring in people's faces, the magistrates demanded of them several times, who it was, of all the people in the room that hurt them. One of the accusers pointed several times at one Captain Hill, but spake nothing. The same accuser had a man standing at her back to hold her up. He stooped down to her ear: then she cried out, Alden, Alden afflicted her. One of the magistrates asked her if she had ever seen Alden. She answered, 'No.' He asked her how she knew it was Alden. She said the man told her so.

"Then all were ordered to go down into the street where a ring was made; and the same accuser cried out, 'There stands Alden, a bold fellow, with his hat on before the judges: he sells powder and shot to the Indians and French, and lies with the Indian squaws, and has Indian papooses.' Then was Alden committed to the marshal's custody, and his sword taken from him; for they said he afflicted them with his sword. After some hours, Alden was sent for to the meetinghouse in the village, before the magistrates, who required Alden to stand upon a chair, to the open view of all the people.

"The accusers cried out that Alden pinched them then, when he stood upon the chair, in the sight of all the people, a good way distant from them. One of the magistrates bid the marshal to hold open Alden's hands that he might not pinch those creatures. Alden asked them why they should think that he should come to that village to afflict those persons that he never knew or saw before. Mister Gedney bid Alden to confess, and give glory to God. Alden said he hoped he should give glory to God, and hoped he should never gratify the Devil: But appealed to all that ever knew him, If they ever suspected him to be such a person; and challenged any one that could bring in any thing on their own knowledge that might give suspicion of his being such a one.

"Mister Gedney said he had known Alden many years, and had been at sea with him, and always looked upon him to be an honest man; but he saw cause to alter his judgment. Alden answered, he was sorry for that, but he hoped God would clear up his innocency that he would recall that judgment again; and added that he hoped that he should, with Job, maintain his integrity till he died. They bid Alden look upon his accusers, which he did, and then they fell down. Alden asked Mister Gedney what reason there could be given why Alden's looking upon him did not strike him down as well; but no reason was given that I heard.

"But the accusers were brought to Alden to touch them; and this touch, they said, made them well. Alden began to speak of the providence of God in suffering these creatures to accuse innocent persons. Mister Noyes asked Alden why he should offer to speak of the providence of God: God, by his providence (said Mister Noyes), governs the world, and keeps it in peace; and so went on with this discourse, And stopped Alden's mouth as to that. Alden told Mister Gedney that he could assure him that there was a lying spirit in them; for I can assure you that there is not a word of truth in all these say of me. But Alden was again committed to the marshal, and his mittimus was written.

"To Boston Alden was carried by a constable: no bail would be taken for him, but was delivered to the prison keeper, where he remained fifteen weeks; and then, observing the manner of trials, and evidence then taken, was at length prevailed with to make his escape." Per, John Alden.

He made good his escape in the middle of September, just before the mass execution of nine convicted witches. Making his way to Duxbury, he took refuge with relatives. When the witch hunt was over, he surrendered, and was delivered to the Superior Court in Boston. On Tuesday, April 25, 1693, he was discharged by proclamation, along with about 150 others.

Governor Phips had left to fight the French and Indians, leaving his lieutenant governor, William Stoughton, and the Council to set up the first session of the Court of Oyer and Terminer. In order to test their authority, they decided to try only one person. Some of the judges must have felt that if the person they picked could be found guilty and the people accepted the verdict, they would have a clear field to continue with the trials.

They must have made a careful study of the early hearings, because the person picked had the right background for conviction. She had been accused of witchcraft on February 25, 1680, and, judging by the fact that she was selling some of her late husband's land in 1691, was acquitted. She was accused a second time, in 1687, by Christian Trask, a woman who had fits of insanity. When the woman came to her senses, she dropped the charges. A short while later Christian committed suicide. The Reverend Hale of Beverly, studied the case and found nothing abnormal in the woman's death. He said no one was to blame for it.

The woman, chosen as the test case, had been running a private inn, where she served cider and entertained men with games of relaxation. Several complaints had been lodged by neighbors over the rowdy goings on at all hours of the night. The name of the woman chosen was Bridget Bishop.

The Attorney General, Thomas Newton, had sent a letter to Isaac Addington, secretary of the province, asking him to send several persons to Salem for trial. He requested Tituba and one other confessed witch as material witnesses. The last part of his request consisted of getting the records for the first persons committed for trial and Bridget Oliver's previous court records from 1680. Bridget Oliver was the name of Bridget Bishop before her marriage to Edward Bishop.

On June 2, Bridget's trial was held. The court's records of the examinations for this and all subsequent trials are missing. However, several depositions and signed testimony are still in existence. The writings of Cotton Mather, Increase Mather, Samuel Sewall, Thomas Hutchinson, Samuel Parris, John Hale, Robert Calef, Deodat Lawson, and others involved in the trials have been gleaned for the events that took place.

The judges on the case were, Nathaniel Saltonstall of Haverhill, Major Bartholomew Gedney of Salem, Major John Richards, Mister Wait Still Winthrop, Captain Samuel Sewall and Mister Peter Sargent, all of Boston. The Chief Justice was Lieutenant Governor William Stoughton. No procedures had been formulated for the crime of witchcraft, leaving the judges no choice but to try the accused under an act of King James I which had been passed in the year 1603.

The evidence presented at the trial was overwhelming, causing the trial to last for six days. I have taken the liberty of presenting a fair amount of it here so the reader can grasp the essence of this historical event. Keep in mind as you read it that the existence of witchcraft was never in question by the Puritan culture. All keepers of the faith accepted it as an absolute fact.

There were five indictments against Bridget Bishop. These indictments charged her with the practice of witchcraft against the bodies of Abigail Williams, Ann Putnam, Mercy Lewis, Elizabeth Hubbard and Mary Walcott. The indictments had the same flavor as the ones mentioned earlier in this book and do not need repeating. Her extensive past history was brought up by the court.

In the year 1670, Bridget and Thomas Oliver were brought before the magistrate for fighting. The complainant was a neighbor by the name of Mary Ropes. The courts were very stringent in that era. The couple was ordered to pay a fine and if payment wasn't made within one month, a public whipping would be held, each of them to receive ten lashes. There is no record of which penalty was imposed.

On December 24, 1677, the couple was again summoned before the court. This time the charge involved Bridget using unacceptable language in public against her husband. This language consisted of using the phrases "old rogue" and "old devil", among others, on the Lord's Day. Found guilty, her punishment was to stand back to back with her husband on Lecture Day for about an hour. The offensive phrases were to be emblazoned on a piece of paper, fastened to each of their foreheads. They were to be gagged for the entire time. It was a custom of the period to punish the husband, along with his wife, for such crimes. It was felt that the husband should have maintained control over his wife at all times.

Thomas Oliver died on June 21, 1679. Bridget gained legal control of the estate in November of that year.

On February 25, 1680, Bridget was arrested on a charge of witchcraft. The charge was brought by a slave named Juan. The man had a strange story to tell.

A month previous, he had been leading a team of horses pulling a sled. Suddenly they reared up and ran into the swamp. Their fright had been such that they became buried up to their bellies. He released the harness and, after much effort, managed to get them out. Some people had seen the horses bolt and made the remark that the horses had acted like they were bewitched.

A week later he went into the hay house to get some hay for the horses. He claimed that he saw the shape of Bridget Oliver standing on a beam with an egg in her hand. He bent down to pick up a pitchfork in order to strike her, but when he uprighted himself, she vanished. He assured the court that the shape was the same as the woman standing before them. He claimed he was so afraid that he ran to the house and told his master what he'd seen.

That night, while he sat eating his dinner, he saw two black cats. Having only one black cat, he was about to ask where the other one had come from, when he felt three sharp pains in his side. He attributed these events to Bridget.

No records of her trial survived, but since she remained a free woman, she must have been found not guilty.

On December 14, 1687, a warrant was issued for Bridget, now married to Edward Bishop. She was arrested on March 6, 1688, on the charge of stealing a piece of brass from the local mill. Thomas Stacey of Salem, owner of the local mill, was her accuser. He claimed that around July of the previous year a brass part had been taken from his mill. Using common sense, he went to Edward Dolbeare's shop to see if someone had sold it to him. At first, Mister Dolbeare denied he had it, but after Thomas Stacey explained that it had been stolen from him, Dolbeare took him to his house to show him what he had. Sure enough, there it was.

When Mister Stacey asked him where he had gotten it, he said that Bridget Bishop's daughter, Christian Mason, had brought it in. Dolbeare said he had asked her where she got it and she replied that it had been laying around the house for some years before her father died. Mister Dolbeare returned the brass part to Thomas Stacey.

Stacey testified that he went over to Edward Bishop's house to make inquiries concerning the matter. He showed Bridget the brass part and asked her to admit her guilt and apologize to him. She got down on her knees and begged his forgiveness, saying she would never do it again. He further testified, at a later date, that she came to the mill and knelt down again, asking the same as she had at home.

Bridget denied stealing the part, or of ever admitting such a thing to Thomas Stacey. She said she'd only talked to him once about it and that was at the mill, where she denied having taken it. John Hathorne, Justice of the Peace, asked her where she had gotten it. She replied that she and her daughter were working in the garden, when her daughter found it. Bridget suggested that her daughter take it to Mister Dolbeare's to find out what it was. She emphasized that she wasn't trying to sell it.

Bridget was bound over for trial. Her husband and William Reeves posted bond. The outcome of this case is missing, but a document written on March 13, 1688, links this case with Bridget's current trial for witchcraft. It reads, "William Stacey of Salem testified that the brass which Bridget Bishop, the wife of Edward Bishop of Salem, sent by her daughter, Christian Mason, to Mister

Dolbeare of Salem, as she acknowledgeth, is the very brass which was stolen out of the mill at Salem last year."

William Stacey was one of her accusers. It is very possible that he didn't like the verdict of her trial for theft and wanted revenge. At her trial for witchcraft, Stacey submitted the following testimony.

"Deposition of William Stacey"

"William Stacey of the town of Salem, aged thirty-six years or thereabouts, deposeth and saith that about fourteen years ago, this deponent was visited with the smallpox. Then Bridget Bishop visited him, and professed a great love for him in his sickness, more than normal, at which he wondered. Some time after the deponent got well, the said Bishop got him to do some work for her, for which she gave him three pence, which seemed to the deponent good pay. He had not gone more than three or four rods (one rod equals sixteen and a half feet) when he looked into his pocket for it, but he could not find it.

"Sometime after, this deponent met the said Bishop in the street going to the mill. She asked this deponent whether his father would grind her grist, he asked her why she asked. She answered, because people thought she was a witch. This deponent answered, he was certain his father would grind it. About six rods away from her, one of this deponent's cart wheels sunk into the ground and he was forced to get help. Returning later he searched, but couldn't find the hole.

"Sometime after, in the winter, about midnight, this deponent felt something cold between his lips, pressing hard against his teeth, it was very cold, and woke him, he sat up in bed. He saw Bridget Bishop sitting at the foot of the bed, at least it seemed to be her, the room was as light as day, she wore a black cape and black hat, and a red coat with two capes of two colors. Then she clasped her coat close to her legs, hopped up on the bed and about the room, then she went out, and the room was dark.

"Again, some time after, the said Bishop came to this deponent and asked if what he'd said about that night was true that he had told several people. He answered that what he said was true, and that it was her, and asked her to deny it if she dared. The said Bishop did not deny it, and went away very angry and said that this deponent did her more mischief that any body. He asked why. She answered, because folks would believe him before anybody else.

"Sometime after, the said Bishop threatened this deponent, and told him he was the one responsible for exposing her as the one who stole the brass.

"Some time after, this deponent on a dark night was going to the barn and was suddenly picked up and thrown against a stone wall and afterwards picked up again and thrown down an embankment at the end of his house.

"Some time after, this deponent met the said Bishop by Isaac Stone's brick kiln. After he had passed by her, the deponent's horse stopped climbing a hill with its small load, the horse strained to go, all its harnessing fell apart and the cart fell down.

"Afterward, this deponent went to lift a bag of corn of about two bushels, but could not budge it with all his might.

"This deponent has met with several other of her pranks at several times, which would take up a great time to tell of.

"This deponent doth verily believe that said Bridget Bishop was instrumental in his daughter Priscilla's death about two years ago. The child was a likely, thriving child, and so screeched out and so continued in an unusual manner for about a fortnight (two weeks), and so died in that lamentable manner."

Earlier in this chapter, I touched on the events of her second witchcraft accusation in 1687. At that time, Reverend John Hale had exonerated her of any wrongdoing. The following is his new testimony, as he gave it at this trial.

"Deposition of the Reverend Mister John Hale"

"John Hale of Beverly, aged about fifty-six years, testifieth and saith that about five or six years ago, Christian, the wife of John Trask (living in Salem bounds bordering on the abovesaid Beverly), being in full communion in our church, came to me to desire that Goodwife Bishop, her neighbor, wife of Edward Bishop, Junior, might not be permitted to receive the Lord's Supper in our church till she had given her, the said Trask, satisfaction for some offenses that were against her; to wit, because the said Bishop did entertain people in her house at unreasonable hours in the night to keep drinking and playing shuffleboard, whereby discord did arise in other families, and young people were in danger to be corrupted.

"And that the said Trask knew these things, and has once gone into the house and finding some at shuffleboard have taken the pieces they play with and thrown them into the fire. and had reproved the said Bishop for promoting such disorders, but received no satisfaction from her about it.

"I gave Christian Trask direction on how to proceed farther in this matter, if it were clearly proved. And indeed, by the information I have had otherwise, I do fear that if a stop had not been put to those disorders, said Edward Bishop's house would have been a house of great profanity and iniquity.

"But as to Christian Trask, the next news I heard of her was that she was insane. And asking her husband, John Trask, when she was so taken, he told me she was taken insane that night after she came from my house when she complained against Goody Bishop.

"She continued some time insane, we sought the Lord by fasting and prayer, and the Lord was pleased to restore the said Trask to the use of her reason again. I was with her often in her insanity and took it then to be only insanity, yet fearing sometimes something yet worse, but since I have seen the fits of those bewitched at Salem Village, I call to mind some of her's to be much like some of theirs.

"The said Trask, when recovered, as I understood it, did manifest strong suspicion that she had been bewitched by the said Bishop's wife, and showed so much averseness from having any conversation with her that I was then troubled at it, As hoping better of Goody Bishop at that time, for we have since [discovered]. At length, said Christian Trask fell again into an insane fit on a Sabbath day, in the morning at the public meeting, creating a public disturbance, and continued, sometimes better, sometimes worse, until her death, manifesting that she was under temptation to kill herself or somebody else.

"I inquired of Margaret King, who stayed at or near the house, what she had observed of said Trask before her last insanity. She told me Goody Trask was much given to reading and searching the prophecies of scripture.

"The day before she made that disturbance in the meeting house, she came home and said she had been with Goody Bishop and that the two of them were now friends, or to that effect.

"I was praying with and counseling Goody Trask before her death, and many days before her end, being there, she seemed more rational, and earnestly desired Edward Bishop might be sent for that she might make friends with him. I asked her if she had wronged Edward Bishop. She said, not that she knew of, unless it were in taking his shuffleboard pieces when people were at play with them and throwing them into the fire. And if she did evil in it, she was very sorry for it, and desired he would be friends with her or forgive her. This was the very day before she died, or a few days before.

"Her insanity (or bewitchment) continued about a month, and in those intervals wherein she was better, she earnestly desired prayers. And the Sabbath before she died, I received a note for prayers on her behalf, which her husband said was written by herself, and I judge was her own handwriting, being well acquainted with her hand.

"As to the wounds she died of, I observed three deadly ones: a piece of her windpipe cut out, and another wound above that, through the windpipe and gullet to the vein they call the jugular. So that I then judged and still do think it impossible for her with so short a pair of scissors to mangle herself so, without some extraordinary work of the Devil or witchcraft."

Samuel Shattuck was the son of a Quaker of the same name. His father had given the government a considerable amount of trouble in his day. Some of his narrow points of view must have rubbed off on his son. Samuel ran a hatter and dyers shop. Bridget would often bring him cloth to dye in bright colors for her decorative wardrobe. Samuel's views on this were very stringent. He felt that a woman's liking of fashionable and colorful clothing was a sign of the Devil. His testimony is given below.

"Deposition of Samuel and Sarah Shattuck"

"Samuel Shattuck aged forty-one years testifieth that in the year 1680, Bridget Oliver formerly wife to old Goodman Oliver; now wife to Edward Bishop, did come to my house pretending to buy an old hood, which though I asked very little for, and for all her pretenses went away without it. And sundry other times she came in a smooth and flattering manner for meaningless things, we have thought since to work mischief.

"At or very near this time, our eldest child, who was healthy and energetic, like any other child of his age, Became sick and the more she came to the house the sicker he got. As he stood in the doorway he would fall out and bruise his face on a large stepping stone, as if he had been pushed by an invisible hand, often times falling and hitting his face in a very miserable manner.

"After this, the above said Oliver brought me a pair of sleeves to dye, and after that sundry pieces of lace, some of which were so short that I could not judge them to be of any use. She paid me two pence for dyeing them, which two pence I gave to Henry Williams who lived with me. He told me he put them in a purse with some other money, which he locked up in a box. And that the purse and money were gone from the box and he didn't know how; and never found it.

"Just after the dyeing of these things, the child had a terrible fit, his mouth and eyes were drawn to one side and he gasped in such a manner that sounded like he was dying. After this his fits grew worse, and because of them he would be constantly crying. For many months he would cry until his strength that nature had given him was gone. Then he would fall asleep and then awaken crying and moaning. To look at him was sad and in time, we could see his understanding decay, so that we feared (as has since been proven) he would loose his mind. Ever since he has been devoid of reason, his fits still follow him.

"After he had been in this kind of sickness some time, he has gone into the garden and climbed up on a board, an inch thick, which lay flat upon the ground. When we called him, he would come to the edge of the board and hold out his hand, and make as if he would come, but could not, till he was helped off the board. Other times, when he got upon the board as aforesaid, my wife has said she has offered him cake and money, if he would come to her. And he has held out his hand and reached for it, but he could not come till he was helped off the board, by which, I judged some enchantment kept him on it.

"About seventeen or eighteen months after this illness first appeared, a stranger came to my house and pitied the child and said among other things, we are all born for something, some for one thing and some for another. I asked him what he thought this child was born for. He replied, he is born to be bewitched. I told him the child was bewitched. He said, he knew and said to me, you have a neighbor that lives nearby, she is a witch. I told him we didn't have any dishonest neighbors. He replied, you have a neighbor that is a witch and she would bring down her wrath on this child.

"I thought to myself and remembered that my wife had told me that Goodwife Oliver had been to the house asking that she beat Henry Williams that lived with us, and that she went away muttering what seemed like threats. It was, but a short time before our child took ill. I told the aforesaid stranger that there was such a woman as he spoke of. He asked where she lived, for he would go and see her if he knew how. I gave him money and bid him to buy a pot of cider for me. I sent my son with him and away he went.

"After a short time, they both returned; the boy's face was bleeding and I asked them what had happened. They told me, the man knocked on the door and Goody Oliver came to the door and asked the stranger, what he wanted. He told her he wanted a pot of cider. She told him, he couldn't have any and asked him to get out. She picked up a spade and made him go out. She followed him out and when she came onto the porch, she saw my small boy, ran up to him, scratched his face and made it bleed; saying to him, 'You rogue, why do you bring this fellow here to plague me?'

"Now this man had said to me before he went; that he would make her draw blood, and ever since this child has been followed with grievous fits, as if he will never recover; his head and eyes drawn to the side, as if they will never straighten out. Also laying down as if he were dead, falling down into fire or water if he is not carefully watched. And generally an uneasy and restless frame of mind, running to and fro, acting so strange that I cannot judge him to be anything but bewitched.

"And by these circumstances, do believe that the aforesaid Bridget Bishop is the cause of it and it has been the judgment of the doctors, both the ones that live here and those from other places that he is under an evil hand of witchcraft."

This has been a cross section of some of the testimony surrounding Bridget Bishop's trial. Her flamboyant character, combined with her actions in public places, were the main things the people were condemning her for. One important fact, previously not mentioned, was that Reverend Noyes, one of the more zealous prosecutors, lived directly across from the Bishops. He was probably one of the biggest complainers against her lifestyle.

On June 8, 1692, Bridget Bishop's verdict was handed down. That will be the opening subject of the next chapter.

CHAPTER IX

THE LULL

June 8, 1692 - July 19, 1692

"To George Corwin, Gentleman, High Sheriff, of the County of Essex. Greeting."

"Whereas Bridget Bishop alias Oliver the wife of Edward Bishop of Salem, in the County of Essex, Sawyer, at a special Court of Oyer and Terminer held at Salem, the second day of this instant month of June, for the Counties of Essex, Middlesex and Suffolk, before William Stoughton Esquire and his Associate Justices of the said Court, was Indicted and arraigned upon several indictments for using, practicing and exercising, on the nineteenth day of April, last, past and diverse other days and times, before and after, certain acts of witchcraft, in and upon the bodies of Abigail Williams, Ann Putnam Junior, Mercy Lewis, Mary Walcott and Elizabeth Hubbard of Salem Village, single women, whereby their bodies were hurt, afflicted, pined, consumed, wasted and tormented, contrary to the form of the statute, in that case made and provided.

"To which Indictments the said Bridget Bishop, pleaded not guilty and for trial thereof, put herself upon God and her Country, where upon she was found guilty of the felonies of witchcraft, whereof she stood Indicted and sentence of Death accordingly passed against her, as the Law directs.

"Execution whereof yet remains to be done.

"These are therefore in the name of their Majesties William and Mary now King and Queen over England &c, to will and command you That upon Friday next, being the tenth day of this instant month of June, between the hours of Eight and twelve in the afternoon of the same day. You safely conduct the said Bridget Bishop alias Oliver, from their Majesties jail in Salem aforesaid, to the place of Execution and there cause her to be hanged by the neck until she be dead, and of your doings herein make return to the Clerk of the said Court and precept.

"And hereof you are not to fail at your peril.

"And this shall be your Sufficient Warrant. Given under my hand and Seal at Boston. The Eighth day of June, in the fourth Year of Reign of our Sovereign Lord and Lady, William and Mary, now King and Queen over England &c; Anno Domini, 1692; William Stoughton."

[Author's note: The above "Death Warrant", is the only one still in existence. It is reproduced with minor corrections in spelling; and the addition of several commas, to overcome the almost total lack of punctuation. As the reader can see, capitalization was also done in a random manner.]

On June 10, Bridget Bishop was hanged, at a place known as Gallows Hill. Sheriff George Corwin made the following notation on the bottom of the warrant.

"June 10, 1692"

"According to the within written precept, I have taken the body of the within named Bridget Bishop, of their Majesties jail in Salem and safely conveyed her to the place provided for her execution and caused the said Bridget to be hanged by the neck until she was dead (and buried in the place), all which was according to the time within required and so I make return by me, George Corwin Sheriff"

The short sentence referring to Bridget's burial, was crossed out. Corwin must have realized that the warrant hadn't told him to bury her.

The trial had been somewhat of a success. I say somewhat because some of the judges weren't quite satisfied with the evidence presented. Judge Nathaniel Saltonstall disliked the way it was handled so much that he resigned. Thomas Danforth was put in his place.

Diaries were popular in those days and, unlike the present, contained true accounts of an individual's daily life. People believed that to tell a lie before God was the condemnation of a man's immortal soul.

For 56 years Judge Samuel Sewall kept such a diary. This diary has proved to be a bonanza for historians. He recorded the peoples names that took their oaths with him on May 24. Then, there is a conspicuous blank between May 24 and July 13. This omission would occur for all but one of the trials in which his college friend was among those executed. It is this author's opinion that Sewall purposefully omitted his comments perhaps because of the volatility of the situation. Later, he would publicly air his true feelings and become the only judge to recant the whole affair.

On June 8 the old colonial law making witchcraft a capital offense was adopted as a law of the province. This took responsibility for the court's decisions away from the place where the trials were held and placed it on the entire population of the country. Before taking a recess, the governor and council solicited the clergy of Boston for an opinion concerning the prosecutions. There wasn't anything unusual in this request; it had been common practice under the old charter.

Their eight-part opinion, as recorded by Thomas Hutchinson, follows.

"The return of several ministers, consulted by his Excellency and the honorable council upon the present witchcraft in Salem Village."

"Boston, June 15, 1692"

"One: The afflicted state of our poor neighbors that are now suffering by molestations from the Invisible World, we apprehend so deplorable that we think their condition calls for the utmost help of all persons in their several capacities.

"Two: We cannot but, with all thankfulness, acknowledge the success which the merciful God has given to the sedulous and assiduous endeavors of our honorable rulers, to defeat the abominable witchcrafts which have been committed in the country, humbly praying that the discovery of those mysterious and mischievous wickednesses may be perfected.

"Three: We judge that in the prosecution of these and all such witchcrafts, there is a need of a very critical and exquisite caution, lest by too much credulity for things received only upon the Devil's authority, there be a door opened for a long train of miserable consequences, and Satan get an advantage over us; for we should not be ignorant of his devices.

"Four: As, in complaints upon witchcraft, there may be matters of enquiry which do not amount unto matters of presumption, and there may be matters of presumption which yet may not be matters of conviction, so it is necessary that all proceedings, thereabout, be managed with an exceeding tenderness towards those that may be complained of, especially if they have been persons of an unblemished nature.

"Five: When the first enquiry is made into the circumstances of such as may fall under the just suspicion of witchcrafts, we could wish that there may be admitted as little as possible of such noise, company and openness as may too hastily expose them that are examined, and that there may be nothing used as a test for the trial of the suspected, the lawfulness whereof may be doubted by the people of God; but that the directions given by such judicious writers, as Perkins and Barnard, may be observed.

"Six: Presumptions whereupon persons may be committed, and, much more, convictions whereupon persons may be condemned, as guilty of witchcrafts, ought certainly to be more considerable than barely the accused person's being represented by a specter unto the afflicted; in as much as it is an undoubted and a notorious thing that a demon may, by God's permission, appear, even to ill purposes, in the shape of an innocent, yes, a virtuous man. Nor can we esteem alterations made in the sufferers, by a look or touch of the accused, to be an infallible evidence of guilt, but frequently liable to be abused by the Devil's evil domain.

"Seven: We know not whether some remarkable affronts given the devils, by our disbelieving those testimonies whose whole force and strength is from them alone, may not put a period unto the progress of the dreadful calamity begun upon us, in the accusation of so many persons, whereof some, we hope, are yet clear from the great transgression laid to their charge.

"Eight: Nevertheless, we cannot but humbly recommend, unto the government, the speedy and vigorous prosecutions, of such as have rendered themselves obnoxious, according to the directions given in the laws of God and the wholesome statutes of the English nation, for the detection of witchcrafts."

This opinion specifically stated that spectral evidence was not acceptable to prove a person's guilt, nor was the sight test or touch test. One of the tests which had great credibility with the judges was the search for the witches mark, better known as a "witches tit." A suspected witch was searched by several people to see if they could find a string wart or some other skin lesion on the private parts of the accused person's body. Most of the accused were aged and, as is natural in such circumstances, many of them had skin blemishes. When the blemish was found, it was pierced with a pin to see if any liquid came out. If so, it was accepted as positive proof of that person's guilt.

The ministers' opinion cautioned the judges against accepting anything other than a confession by the accused, or actual proof of a supernatural act. The seventh finding was a plea, made in vain, for common sense. The judges seem to have ignored all but the eighth finding, which they followed with a great deal of vigor. One interesting point that the ministers made was in Finding Four. It was the presumption of a person's innocence until proven guilty. This was in contradiction to English criminal law, and is the basis of our modern legal system.

On June 16, Roger Toothaker, died in Boston prison. He had

been arrested for witchcraft on May 28.

When the judges returned from adjournment on June 28, Sarah Good, Rebecca Nurse, Elizabeth Howe, Sarah Wilds and Susanna Martin, were brought in for trial.

Sarah Good was the poor homeless creature who had lost her newborn child in prison and shared her cell with her little daughter Dorcas. The testimony against her was, like that of Bridget Bishop, mostly comprised of character assassination and superstitious nonsense. Some examples follow.

Samuel Abbey and his wife Mary testified that about three years earlier, William Good and his wife Sarah had no place to live. Out of kindness, the Abbeys gave them a place to stay. Their charity ran thin when Sarah's violent temper began to flair at regular intervals. The Abbeys finally threw them out. Sarah treated them very spitefully after this episode. That winter their cattle started dying from an unknown malady. Within two years they had lost seventeen head of cattle, several pigs and several hogs.

William Good came home one day and told Sarah about the great calamity that had befallen the Abbeys. She responded that she didn't care if they lost all of their cattle. John Good repeated this to the Abbeys. They concluded that Sarah Good was responsible for their misery and that she had bewitched their animals.

Sarah Gadge, the wife of Thomas Gadge, said that 2 1/2 years ago, Sarah Good came to her house and wanted to come in. Sarah Gadge told her she couldn't come in, because she didn't know where Sarah Good had been, and she might have picked up smallpox at one of her questionable places. Sarah Good muttered something and became very angry. She told Sarah Gadge that if she didn't let her in, she'd give her something to worry about. Sarah Gadge told her she wanted nothing to do with her.

The next morning one of Sara Gadge's cows died in a mysterious manner. She attributed its death to Sarah Good. Thomas Gadge, her husband, corroborated her story.

William Good said that the night before Sarah was to be examined for witch marks, he saw a wart, or "witch's tit," just below her right shoulder. He had never seen it before and had asked the examiners if they saw it the next day.

Samuel Braybrook said that when he brought Sarah Good to Ipswich jail, she jumped from her horse three times. At that same instant, Ann Putnam Junior, who was at home in Salem village, declared that she saw her do it. (The court didn't even ask him how he knew Ann had done this. He was several miles away at the time.) He went on to say that Sarah told him she wanted to kill herself.

One of the afflicted girls had a fit. When she came out of it she yelled that Sarah Good stabbed her with a knife. She said the blade broke off. With that, the judges searched her for the broken blade. A young man stood up in the court and said she was lying. He had broken his knife yesterday and the afflicted girl had been standing close to him at the time. The young man produced the other half of the knife. The two halves were compared. The judges told the girl not to lie, yet continued to accept her testimony.

Sarah Good was found guilty and sentenced to be hung.

Sarah Wilds, a humble and religious woman, had been accused by the afflicted girls. Some of her other accusers are worthy of mention.

John Andrew (37) and Joseph Andrew (33) claimed that 18 years earlier they had asked Sarah Wilds if they could borrow a scythe to cut down some of their hay. She said no; she didn't have one. A neighbor who was standing there at the time, interrupted and said John Wilds Junior's scythe was hanging from a tree in the yard. The two men walked over to it and took it. They walked back to the house and told Sarah they would ask John when they found him if it was alright for them to borrow it. Sarah was very angry and said it was a sorry world when people could do whatever they pleased.

The two men took it in spite of her objections. Sarah's little boy, Ephraim, caught up to them and told them his mother said they'd better bring it back or else they would pay dearly. The two men ignored the little boy and went on with their work. After they were finished they loaded their ox-drawn cart and headed home. One disaster after another befell the overloaded cart. The brothers decided that Sarah Wilds had bewitched it.

Elizabeth Symonds testified that twelve or thirteen years previous she was walking with her mother, Misses Andrew, in Topsfield. They were on their way to visit Misses Reddington. Sarah Wilds caught up to them and asked them to return her son's scythe. Misses Andrew told Sarah about all the trouble her sons had getting the load of hay home. Sarah replied, "It may be, but I know nothing about it." Misses Andrew asked why Sarah had threatened them, telling them they had better leave the scythe alone. Sarah denied that it was a threat and asked her to prove that it was.

Elizabeth Symonds went on to describe several natural occurrences, including what appears to have been a dream. She related all of this to witchcraft on the part of Sarah Wilds.

The discrepancy in the dates of these two pieces of testimony went unnoticed by the judges. Despite all the testimony in support of her good character, Sarah Wilds was pronounced guilty and sentenced to death.

Susanna Martin, widow, of Amesbury, was the short, slightly plump woman arrested on April 30. Her most distinguishing feature was her neatness. She was a woman that spoke her mind with intelligence. During her hearing on May 2, she had no problem telling the girls what she thought of their antics.

Robert Downer had the most convincing story for the judges. He claimed that several years ago she had threatened him by saying that a she-devil would come and drag him away. Two people came forward and corroborated his story.

Sarah Atkinson said that during very fowl weather, Susanna Martin came to her door. Sarah let Susanna in. Sarah asked her how she came there and Susanna answered that she had walked. Sarah thought Susanna must be soaking wet and asked her if she'd like to dry off by the fire. Susanna said she was perfectly dry and rolled her coat back to expose her shoes. To Sarah's surprise, Susanna's shoes were completely dry. Sarah remarked that if it had been her she would have had water up to her knees. Susanna replied that she disliked having wet clothes.

John Atkinson testified that, five years previous, he traded a cow he had gotten from Reverend Wells to one of Susanna's sons. The son picked up the cow at Wells' house. When John Atkinson went to get his cow, Susanna Martin muttered and didn't want him to take it. He took it anyway. On the way to his home, the cow became cantankerous, and, breaking away, ended up in the river. John had to go into the river to retrieve it. When he got the cow onto the boat, it calmed down.

Neither John or Sarah Atkinson claimed the events had anything to do witchcraft. The judges, in their wisdom, condemned Susanna Martin to death.

Elizabeth Howe was the woman whose blind husband and family had fought so hard to save her. The two ministers submitted their testimony, saying the little Perley girl had been prompted to say that Elizabeth had afflicted her. Several testimonies were submitted attesting to Elizabeth's exemplary character, but it was of no use. She was convicted and sentenced to hang.

Rebecca Nurse was the last to be tried. She was the matronly old woman against whom Thomas Putnam's wife cried out. She was the first of the well-respected women accused. Her trial was a lengthy one. Before the trials began, on June 28, Rebecca petitioned the court;

"To the Honored Court of Oyer and Terminer, now sitting in Salem, this twenty-eighth of June, 1692"

"The humble petition of Rebecca Nurse of Salem Village, humbly asks:

"That whereas some women searched your petitioner at Salem, as I understood for some supernatural mark, and then one of the said women who is known to be, the most ancient, skillful, prudent person of all the ones involved, did Express herself to be, of the opposite opinion from the rest and did then declare that she saw nothing on or about your Honors poor petitioner, but what might arise from a natural cause.

"And I gave the said persons sufficient reason for my problem, which was caused by extreme weakness; coming on partly from an act of nature and difficult stress that has befallen me in my times of travail.

"And therefore your petitioner humbly prays that your Honors would be pleased to send in some other women to enquire into this great problem, Those that are very wise and skillful; namely Misses Higginson Senior, Misses Buckstone, Misses Woodberry two of these being midwives, Misses Porter together with such others, as may be chosen, on that account, before I am Brought to my trial. All which I hope your Honors, will take into your prudent consideration, and find it quite so to do, for my life is now in your hands under God.

"And being conscious of my own innocence, I humbly beg that I may have liberty to prove it to the world partly by the abovesaid. And your poor petitioner shall evermore pray as in duty bound &c".

Her daughters presented a statement on her behalf.

"We whose names are underwritten, can testify, if called to it, That Goody Nurse has been troubled with an infirmity of the body for many years, which the jury of women seem to be afraid it should be something else."

There are no examination records for Rebecca after this date. It is very likely that the court ignored the petition.

Several people who had watched in silence as the others were tried came forth and testified in Rebecca's behalf.

Nathaniel Putnam, the brother of Thomas Putnam's father, had supported the witch trials, but he couldn't bring himself to believe Rebecca was guilty. The following document was found, but it's not certain if it was admitted into evidence.

"Nathaniel Putnam, Senior, being desired of Francis Nurse, Senior, to give information of what I could say concerning his wife's life and conversation, I, the abovesaid, have known this aforesaid woman forty years, and what I have observed of her, human frailties excepted, her life and conversation have been according to her faith; and she has brought up a large family of children and educated them well, so that there is in some of them a great deal of godliness. I have known her to argue with her neighbors; but I never knew or heard of any that did accuse her of what she is now charged with."

Another document which was believed to have been admitted was this one, signed by thirty-nine of the most prominent people in Salem Village, eight of the signatures were from the Putnam family.

"We whose names are hereunto subscribed, being desired by Francis Nurse to declare what we know concerning his wife's conversation for past time; we can testify, to all whom it may concern that we have known her for many years; and, according to our observation, her life and conversation were according to her religion, and we never had any grounds to suspect her of any such thing as she is now accused of."

It is interesting to note that Jonathan Putnam and his wife Lydia signed this paper. He had been one of the two who had taken out the original warrant for Rebecca's arrest. This document should have saved her life.

To the surprise of the judges, the jury came in with a verdict of not guilty. The accusers made a ruckus about it. The prosecutors and the court expressed their dissatisfaction to the jury. They were ordered to reconsider, a thing unheard of in a not-guilty verdict. They returned a second verdict of guilty.

On July 3, the Reverend Noyes took away the only thing Rebecca had left to her. He had the unmitigated gall to have her carried to the meetinghouse so that he could do it to her in the public eye. Thomas Hutchinson expressed what went on in the following words.

"Mister Noyes, the minister of Salem, a zealous prosecutor, excommunicated the poor old woman, and delivered her to Satan, to whom he supposed she had formally given herself to, many years before; but her life and conversation had been such that the remembrance thereof, in a short time after, wiped off all the reproach occasioned by the civil or ecclesiastical sentence against her."

Thomas Fisk was the foreman of the jury. Below is an explanation of the verdict that he gave to some of Rebecca's relatives.

"July 4, 1692"

"I Thomas Fisk the subscriber hereof, being one of them that were the jury last week at Salem court, upon the trial of Rebecca Nurse, &c, being desired, by some of the relations, to give a reason why the jury brought her in guilty, after the verdict not guilty. I do hereby give my reasons as follows.

"When the verdict, not guilty, was given, the honored court was pleased to object against it, saying to the jury that they think the jury let slip the words which the prisoner at the bar spoke against herself, which were spoken in reply to Deliverance Hobbs and her daughter, who had been faulty in setting their hands to the Devil's book as they had formerly confessed. The words were, 'What? Do these persons give in evidence against me now? They use to come among us.' After the honored court had manifested their dissatisfaction with the verdict, several of the jury declared themselves desirous to go out again, and thereupon the honored court gave leave. But, when we came to consider the case, I could not tell how to take her words as an evidence against her, till she had a further opportunity to explain them, if she would take it. And then going into court, I mentioned the words aforesaid, which by one of the court were affirmed to have been spoken by her, she was at the bar but made no reply nor explained them; whereupon these words were to me the principal evidence against her. Thomas Fisk"

Her silence to the foreman's question had forced the jury to find her guilty. When Rebecca found out what had happened she wrote a declaration to the court.

"These presents do humbly show, to the honored Court and Jury that I being informed that the Jury brought me in as guilty, upon my saying that Goodwife Hobbs and her daughter were of our company. But I intended no other way, than as they were prisoners with us, and therefore did then, and yet do judge them not legal evidence against their fellow prisoners. And I being somewhat hard of hearing, and full of grief, no one informing me how the court took up my words, and therefore did not have the opportunity to declare what I meant, when I said they were in my company. Rebecca Nurse"

Her plea was ignored.

Several petitions were submitted for some of the women. Rebecca Nurse was given a reprieve by the Governor. As soon as word got around, her accusers started complaining of her again.

There was a private organization of well-to-do "gentlemen" that had been formed in Salem. Their whole purpose was to ferret out accused witches and see that they were properly punished. They must have been very powerful men. After a private talk with the Governor, he withdrew his reprieve for Rebecca.

On July 19, 1692, the five women were marched up Gallows Hill. It must have been a pitiful sight. Some of them were too old and infirm to make the climb up the rocky slope.

There is only one recorded event of that day. As the noose was being placed around Sarah Good's neck, the Reverend Noyes was still trying to get her to confess by saying such things as, "You are a witch; you know you are a witch." She looked him square in the eye and said, "You are a liar! I am no more a witch than you are a wizard; and, if you take away my life, God will give you blood to drink!" With those words she died, leaving poor scared little Dorcas with no one to care for her.

Thomas Hutchinson said that her prediction seems to have come true. It is traditionally believed that the Reverend Noyes died in 1717 of an internal hemorrhage which caused him to bleed profusely from his mouth. He choked to death on his own blood.

Of the others, I'm sure Elizabeth Howe's husband and daughters were there in her last moments. Being a gentle woman with an inner peace that comes with pure devotion, she probably accepted her fate with the dignity she displayed in everyday life.

Sarah Wilds probably accepted it in the same way as Elizabeth Howe.

Susanna Martin, most likely, let every one know exactly what she thought of the whole affair, in no uncertain terms.

Rebecca probably went in a daze, disbelieving the cruelty of the past weeks, but thankful for her faith.

The bodies were thrown into a crevasse and thinly covered over by the executioners.

Rebecca's husband, sons, and sons-in-law snuck back to Gallows Hill and removed her body from its shallow grave. Her remains were placed in a grave next to where her husband and children would be buried, when their time came.

CHAPTER X

MORE MARTYRS

July 19, 1692 - August 19, 1692

The hangings on July 19 were a disgrace to all concerned. During the trial an incident occurred that would start to put doubts into the minds of many. One of the afflicted girls, in an attempt to get more attention for herself, cried out against a new person. The person's name was Reverend Samuel Willard of the Old South Church. The judges were shocked at this accusation and shuffled the girl out of the room as quickly as possible. The girl had picked on the wrong man; his religious leadership was beyond reproach. The prosecutors told the audience that she had obviously been mistaken, getting the Reverend's name mixed up with that of John Willard, one of the accused.

This incident, plus the improper way Rebecca Nurse's verdict had been handled, made several people in authority start to wonder in private if the whole thing might be an horrendous mistake. [Historical note: Reverend Samuel Willard became vice president of Harvard.]

On July 30, Judge Samuel Sewall made an entry in his diary. "Misses Cary makes her escape out of Cambridge Prison, who was committed for witchcraft." Although he was a judge at the hearings and the trials, this is only his second mention of witchcraft. The first was on April 11: "Went to Salem where, in the meetinghouse, the persons accused of witchcraft were examined; was a very great assembly; 'twas awful to see how the afflicted persons were agitated. Mister Noyes prayed at the beginning, and Mister Higginson concluded." At a later date he wrote in the margin, "Alas, alas, alas, witchcraft."

By August 1, enough people had confronted the ministers of New England concerning the travesty of justice that took place on July 19 to force them to call a general meeting. Increase Mather and seven other ministers gathered at Cambridge to discuss the witch trials. The ministers were very disappointed in the court for having ignored their written opinions two months before. The ministers asked Increase Mather to write a book, putting these opinions into a more forceful form. The book, titled *Cases of Conscience Concerning Evil Spirits*, wasn't published until November.

In order to get it into the hands of the people in power as quickly as possible, a copy of the manuscript was presented to Governor Phips as well as several hand-written copies which were circulated by early October. The reader should not think that the ministers were disclaiming witchcraft. Quite to the contrary, they believed with absolute faith in such things. They disagreed with the methods used by the court and felt that many pious people were being wrongfully condemned for what appeared to be neighborly disputes and personal revenge.

On August 4, news reached New England about the devastating earthquake that had hit Jamaica on June 7 in which 1700 people lost their lives.

On August 5, the Court of Oyer and Terminer was back in session. Six people were brought before the bench: Reverend George Burroughs, John Willard, George Jacobs Senior, Martha Carrier, John Proctor, and his wife, Elizabeth Proctor.

Martha Carrier was the outspoken mother of four, whose children had been coerced into testifying that she was a witch. She had been arrested on March 28, and at her hearing she had directly accused the afflicted children of lying. This incensed them to increase their complaints against her. Methodically, they would complain to Thomas and John Putnam that Goody Carrier bit and pinched them. This and various torturous behavior went on until she was brought to trial.

Elizabeth Hubbard, Mary Walcott, Thomas Putnam, and John Putnam each submitted new testimony just before Martha's trial. Most of the other complaints were directly related to land disputes, normally a civil matter. But in this disagreement, positive proof of witchcraft was claimed.

The early months of 1692 were plagued by drought. For this reason crops failed and animals died of malnutrition and dehydration. Superstitious people, unable to grasp nature, blamed it on the first person they thought of who had been at odds with them. Hence, most of the complaints against these innocent souls came as a direct result of an earlier squabble.

Martha Carrier was condemned to death.

George Burroughs, the humble minister from the colonies,

gave a valiant fight in court. When he was asked how he'd managed to beat a wagon home when the driver had testified that no normal man could have done it, he said a black man had accompanied him on that particular occasion. He explained that they took several short cuts and that the two of them arrived long before the wagon. The accusers said that the Devil was in the form of a black man at the time.

His feats of strength were used to corroborate the accusers' stories. Being a small man, no one believed he had the strength of an iron monger. He had lifted a seven-foot long shotgun, using only one finger stuffed down the barrel, holding it at arm's length for several seconds. Another feat reported to the court was the carrying of a barrel of cider from a boat to the shore using two fingers inserted into the small hole on its top. George Burroughs' response to this was that an Indian who was there did the same thing. His accusers responded that the Devil had taken on the form of an Indian. No matter what he said, his accusers twisted it against him.

The afflicted made a great commotion, guaranteeing a verdict of guilty. One interesting thing about this case is the preponderance of evidence submitted after his execution. Several depositions were entered into his record posthumously. It is believed that the prosecutors felt that they could justify his death by loading his file with false accusations. One of these depositions was written by a man named James Greenslit. His summons to give evidence was written and served on July 26. Cotton Mather claimed that Greenslit had been persuaded by others not to show up for the trial. Six weeks after George Burroughs' trial, Greenslit came to be with his mother (Ann Pudeator) during her trial. Between the time of her conviction and the time of her execution, he wrote his deposition against George Burroughs. The date at the bottom was September 15, seven days before his mother was to die. Apparently he wrote it, possibly under coercion, in the vain hope that it might somehow save his mother. His deposition repeated the shotgun and cider barrel story, combining them into one incident.

John Willard was the constable who had spoken out against the treatment of the accused prisoners he'd arrested.

Two of the pieces of evidence at his trial were discourses on John Willard's beating of his wife. One of them complained of hearing a strange noise in the middle of the night. John had explained that it was locusts, but the person making the complaint became afraid when he heard the noise again a few nights later.

Susanna Sheldon, one of the afflicted, had the longest deposition against him. She accused him of the deaths of three people

107

and stated that one night she saw two black pigs sucking on his breasts.

The Wilkins family came out in force against him. They were the ones that blamed John for Bray Wilkins' heart attack and Daniel Wilkins' death. By the time they were finished with him, they had added the death of Lydia Wilkins and accused his specter of pushing Samuel Wilkins off his horse.

John Willard was sentenced to death.

George Jacobs Senior was the exceptionally tall, elderly man that walked with two canes. One of the afflicted girls, Sarah Churchill, had broken down after the first day of his hearing, telling Misses Ingersoll how the girls had put her up to it.

George Jacobs Junior had fled with Daniel Andrew, leaving his wife, Rebecca, and their children to fend for themselves. Rebecca was not very sane and confessed to being a witch. Margaret was her oldest daughter, as mentioned in Chapter VI. Her first hearing transcripts have been lost to time. Reverend Noyes, whose function seems to have been to force confessions out of the prisoners, succeeded in breaking down Margaret, who had a weak, frightened character, and she confessed herself to be a witch thus leaving George Jacobs Senior without any defense at his trial. Heartbroken, he resigned himself to his fate. In his old age he had been condemned to die for a crime that he believed no one could commit, and by his own family at that.

After his trial on August 12, he drew up a new will. He did this because his daughter-in-law and granddaughter had proved themselves too weak to have the responsibility of such a large estate. He named his son George as executor of his estate and secured its succession to male offspring. While he was doing this, unknown to him, his granddaughter, Margaret, wrote the following declaration:

"The humble declaration of Margaret Jacobs unto the honored court now sitting at Salem, showeth that whereas your poor and humble declarant being closely confined here in Salem jail for the crime of witchcraft, which crime thanks be to God I am innocent of, as will appear at the great day of judgment.

"May it please the honored court, I was cried out upon by some of the possessed persons, as afflicting them; whereupon I was brought in for examination, which persons at the sight of me fell down, which did very much startle and scare me.

"The Lord above knows I knew nothing, in the least measure, of how or who afflicted them; they told me, without a doubt I did, or else they would not fall down at me; they told me, if I would not confess, I should be put down into the dungeon and would be hanged, but if I confess I would save my life; the which did so scare me, with my own vile and wicked heart, into saving my life; it made me make the confession I did, which confession, may it please the honored court, is altogether false and untrue.

"The very first night after I had made the confession, I was in such horror of conscience that I could not sleep, for fear the Devil should carry me away, for telling such horrid lies.

"I was, may it please the court, sworn to my confession, as I understand since, but, at the time, I was ignorant of it, not knowing what an oath meant. The Lord, I hope, in whom I trust, out of the abundance of his mercy, will forgive me, my false swearing of myself.

"What I said, was altogether false against my grandfather, and Mister Burroughs, which I did to save my life and have my liberty; but the Lord, charging it to my conscience, made me in so much horror that I could not contain myself before I had denied my confession, which I did though I saw nothing but death before me, choosing rather death with a clear conscience, than to live in such horror, which I could not allow.

"Where, upon my denying my confession, I was committed to close confinement in prison, where I have enjoyed a more felicitous spirit, a thousand times, than I did before I told the truth.

"And now, may it please your honors, your declarant, having, in part, given your honors a description of my condition, do leave it to your honors pious and judicious discretions, to take pity and compassion on my young and tender years, to act and do with me, as the Lord above and your honors shall see good, having no friend, but the Lord, to plead my cause for me; not being guilty in the least measure of witchcraft, nor any other sin that deserves death from man; and your poor humble declarant shall forever pray, as she is bound in duty, for your honors happiness in this life and eternal felicity in the world to come.

"So prays your honors declarant. Margaret Jacobs."

She read her confession before the court. Predictably her testimony was ignored and she was thrown into the dungeon.

The day after her grandfather was executed, Margaret wrote the following letter to her father.

"From the Dungeon in Salem Prison, August 2, 1692."

"Honored Father, after my humble duty remembered to you, hoping in the Lord of your good health, as, blessed be God! I am joyous, though in abundance of affliction, being close confined here in a loathsome dungeon. The Lord look down in mercy upon me, not knowing how soon I shall be put to death, by means of the afflicted persons, my grandfather having suffered already, and all his estate seized by the King. The reason of my confinement is this; I having, through the magistrates threats, and my own vial and wretched heart, confessed several things contrary to my conscience and knowledge, though to the wounding of my own soul; the Lord pardon me for it!

"But, oh! The terrors of a wounded conscience, who can bear it? But, blessed be the Lord! He would not let me go on in my sins, but in mercy, I hope, to my soul, would not suffer me to keep it any longer; But, I was forced to confess the truth before the magistrates, who would not believe me; but it is their pleasure to put me in here, and God knows how soon I shall be put to death.

"Dear Father, let me beg your prayers to the Lord on my behalf, and send us a joyful and happy meeting in heaven. My mother, poor woman, is very crazy, and remembers her kind love to you, and to uncle; i.e., Daniel Andrew. [Author's note: It is a European custom to allow your children to think of your close friends as 'uncle' or 'aunt'.] So, leaving you to the protection of the Lord, I rest, your dutiful daughter. Margaret Jacobs."

Margaret became ill after writing this and was unable to stand trial in September. By the time her trial was to be held, the witch hunt had subsided in its ferocity.

She had asked if she could see George Burroughs, the day before his execution. Permission was granted. She confessed what she had done to him and asked his forgiveness. He gave it gladly and prayed with her. On that same day she visited her grandfather and had the same discussion as with George Burroughs. After she left her grandfather, he had his will brought to him. In the space that separated two paragraphs, he wrote a clause giving his granddaughter a legacy of ten pounds to be paid in silver.

Because George Jacobs Senior had been given a sentence of death, he was stripped of all his civil rights, making this will null and void. It became one more fragment of the courts records. Almost 20 years later the General Court, finding out the circumstances surrounding the clause, elected to honor it and gave Margaret ten pounds from the Province treasury.

John Proctor was the man that had accompanied his wife, Elizabeth, to her hearing and had become so outraged with the antics of the accusers that he had become a victim. He could see the conspiracy between the afflicted girls from the very beginning and felt their accusations were deliberate and criminal.

Before his trial began, he made his will. He knew that if a man made out the proper document before he was convicted of a capitol offense, Sheriff Corwin wouldn't be able to touch his estate. Then on July 23, he sat down and wrote a letter to five men he felt were sympathetic to the people in prison.

Reverend Increase Mather was the most important minister in Massachusetts and he had extremely powerful connections. Increase's only fault was that he couldn't accept George Burroughs' feats of strength as natural. To his dying day he felt Burroughs was guilty. In most other cases he thought the evidence used for conviction was unacceptable.

Reverend James Allen of the First Church of Boston took an early, leading role in opposing the party that had supported the witch trials. His influence almost saved Rebecca Nurse. His deep-rooted friendship with Increase Mather sometimes helped to keep Cotton Mather in check.

Reverend Joshua Moody of the First Church of Boston had influence that resulted in the successful escape of Phillip English and his wife from the Boston jail. He had spent a considerable time in prison in a fight defending his beliefs in freedom of religion.

Reverend Samuel Willard of the Old South Church of Boston was one of the most revered ministers in the country. His extensive publications were considered to be of very high caliber. John Proctor probably picked him because one of the afflicted girls had accused him at the last trial. John knew this would plant the seed of doubt in this brilliant minister's mind.

Reverend John Bailey of the First Church of Boston. He suffered religious repression in England and made his way to New England, where he gained the utmost respect of his fellow clergymen.

As was his character, John wrote this letter to include the plight of his fellow prisoners. The document stands out, giving us insight into the conditions the prisoners faced during their long ordeal:

"Reverend Gentlemen, the innocency of our case, with the enmity of our accusers and our judges and jury, whom nothing but our blood will serve, having condemned us before our trials, being so much incensed and enraged against us by the Devil, makes us bold to beg and implore your favorable assistance of this our humble petition to His Excellency that if it be possible our innocent blood may be spared, Which undoubtedly otherwise will be shed, if the Lord does not mercifully step in.

"The magistrates, ministers, juries and all the people in general, being so much enraged and incensed against us by the delusion of the Devil, which we can term no other, from that which we know, in our own consciences, we are all innocent persons.

"There are five persons who have recently confessed themselves to be witches, and do accuse some of us of being along with them at a sacrament, since we were committed into close imprisonment, which we know to be lies. Two of the five are young men (Martha Carrier's sons), who would not confess anything till they tied them neck and heels, till the blood was ready to come out of their noses; and it is credibly believed and reported that this was the occasion of making them confess what they never did, by reason they said one had been a witch a month, and the other five weeks, and that their mother made them so, who has been confined here this nine weeks.

"My son, William Proctor, when he was examined, because he would not confess that he was guilty, when he was innocent, they tied him neck and heels until the blood gushed out at his nose, and would have kept him so 24 hours, if someone, more merciful than the rest, had not taken pity on him, and caused him to be unbound.

"These actions are very like the Popish cruelties. They have already undone us in our estates, and that will not serve their turns without our innocent blood. If it cannot be granted that we can have our trials in Boston, we humbly beg that you would endeavor to have these magistrates changed, and others put in their place; begging also and beseeching you that you would be pleased to be here, if not all, some of you, at our trials, hoping thereby you may be the means of saving the shedding of our innocent blood.

"Desiring your prayers to the Lord in our behalf, we rest, your poor afflicted servants. John Proctor, etc."

The phrase, "Popish cruelties", was a direct reference to the Inquisition, one of the main things that had brought people to America. The ministers did what they could to help, but their efforts were in vain.

This letter was probably read by the prosecutors before being sent to the ministers. Combined with John Proctor's frank outspokenness, it created a hatred so strong that all of his family above the age of infancy and most of his wife's relatives were accused and thrown into prison. The infants were left with no one to take care of them, and the house was stripped clean by Sheriff George Corwin.

The decision had been made to convict him, no matter what his defense might be. The afflicted threw everything they had at him, but the evidence in his favor was overwhelming. His friends rallied to his support and two documents were submitted signed by the most prominent names in the area. The first was written by the Reverend John Wise. It contained thirty-two signatures beginning with his.

"The Humble and Sincere Declaration of us, Subscribers, Inhabitants of Ipswich, on Behalf of our Neighbors, John Proctor and his Wife, now in Trouble and under Suspicion of Witchcraft.

"To the honorable Court of Assistants now sitting in Boston. Honored and Rightful Worshipful, the aforesaid John Proctor may have great reason to justify the Divine Sovereignty of God under these severe remarks of Providence upon his peace and honor, under a due reflection upon his life past; and the best of us have reason to adore the great pity and indulgence of God's providence that we are not exposed to the utmost shame the Devil can invent, under the permissions of his sovereignty, though for that sin forenamed, yet for our many transgressions.

"For we do at present suppose that it may be a method within the severe but just transactions of the infinite majesty of God that he sometimes may permit Satan to impersonate, make crazy, and thereby abuse innocents and such as do, in the fear of God, defy the Devil and all his works. The great rage he allowed in the temptation of Job; the abuse he did to Samuel in disturbing his grave, by using his specter in answer to the charms of witchcraft; and other instances from good hands, may be used for argument.

"Besides the unsearchable footsteps of God's judgments that are brought to light every morning that astonish our weaker reasons; to teach us adoration, trembling, dependence, etc. But we must not trouble Your Honors by being tedious. Therefore being smitten with the notice of what has happened, we reckon it within the duties of our charity that teaches us to do unto others as we would have done unto us, to offer thus much for the clearing of our neighbors innocency; i.e. that we never had the least knowledge of such a nefarious wickedness in our said neighbors, since they have been in our acquaintance.

"Neither do we remember any such thoughts in us concerning them, or any action by them, or either of them, directly tending that way, no more than might be in the lives of any other persons of the clearest reputation, as to any such evils. What God may have left them to, we cannot go into God's pavilion clothed with clouds of darkness round about; but, as to what we have ever seen or heard of them, upon our consciences we judge them innocent of the crime accused.

"He was born among us, and came from religious parents in our place, and, by reason of relations and properties within our town, has had constant conversation with us. We speak upon our personal acquaintance and observation; and so we leave our neighbors, and this our testimony on their behalf, to the wise thoughts of Your Honors."

113

The second document was written by Nathaniel Felton Senior. Half of the section containing the signatures was purposefully cut away with a pair of scissors. Maybe someone didn't want a name to be discovered as opposing the trial. At any rate the total signatures is estimated to be around forty. None of the signatures duplicate those on the first document.

"We, whose names are underwritten, having several years known John Proctor and his wife, do testify that we never heard or understood that they were ever suspected to be guilty of the crime now charged upon them; and several of us, being their near neighbors, do testify that, to our apprehension, they lived Christian-like in their family, and were ever ready to help such as stood in need of their help."

Evidence was introduced, showing that one of the afflicted girls denied the testimony she'd given in court. She said she must have been "out of her head", and that she never meant to accuse them. Another was caught in a lie and admitted that her accusation was false. She said that the girls did it in fun, just for sport.

It appears, at least to this author, that John and Elizabeth were tried together. The evidence seems to indicate that Elizabeth's verdict depended on convicting John. In spite of overwhelming evidence in their favor, they were sentenced to hang. The decision was short lived when it was discovered that Elizabeth was in her last months of pregnancy. Her sentence was postponed until she made delivery of the innocent child. Two weeks after her husband was hanged, she gave birth in her cell. By the time her case came around again, she, like Margaret Jacobs, would not have to be executed. It was ironic that by a strange twist of fate her life had been spared, and her husband's had been taken.

After John Proctor's conviction, he asked for time to make arrangements for his family and business. His request was denied. Mister Noyes refused to pray with him unless he confessed to witchcraft. John would not bend in his principles.

On August 19, the five prisoners were put in a large wooden cart and taken to Gallows Hill.

Martha Carrier, like all that went before or since, professed her innocence and faith. I have no doubt, she admonished the afflicted children as liars one last time. Then, saying a prayer, she died.

John Willard and John Proctor carried themselves with great deportment as they walked to the gallows. They looked saintly and left a disturbing impression of innocence on the crowd's mind.

George Jacobs Senior, after saying a prayer, died quietly. His body is the only one whose location is certain. One of his grandsons somehow procured the body and, strapping it to a horse, brought it back to George's farm and buried it under the trees. In 1864, the body was exhumed for examination. The bones were checked and found to have belonged to an exceptionally tall man, fitting the descriptions given in the books written during the trials. When the study was concluded, George Jacobs Senior was laid back to rest where he remains to this day.

George Burroughs died as he had lived, fighting for what he believed. When he climbed up the ladder to receive the noose around his neck, he stopped and gave a speech defending his innocence. After the speech, he prayed, ending his prayer with a perfect recital of the Lord's Prayer. The crowd became restless; they had been told that a witch couldn't say the Lord's Prayer without a mistake. George had said it with a force and reverence that astonished them. Some of the accusers said that the black man was standing next to him telling him what to say. Before anyone could react to all of this, George Burroughs was hanged.

Afterwards Cotton Mather, feeling that Burroughs had gotten the better of him, said that Burroughs was no minister. The Devil, he said, often transformed himself into an angel of light. The people seemed to accept this explanation.

George Burroughs was cut down and dragged to a rocky crack in the ground. His shirt and pants were torn off and the pants of one of the other victims was put on. His body was dumped in with Martha Carrier and John Willard. Their burial was so sloppily handled that one of George's hands, his chin and one of the other victims feet were left exposed.

Judge Samuel Sewall remained silent no longer. The death of his college friend was too hard to bear. He wrote the following in his diary:

"This day, George Burroughs, John Willard, John Proctor, Martha Carrier and George Jacobs were executed in Salem, a very great number of spectators being present. Mister Cotton Mather was there, Mister Sims, Hale, Noyes, Cheever, etc. All of them said they were innocent, Carrier and all. Mister Mather says they all died by a righteous sentence. Mister Burroughs by his speech, prayer, protestation of his innocence, did much move unthinking persons, which occasioned them to speak harshly about his being executed."

In the margin, he wrote, "Doleful! Witchcraft!"

CHAPTER XI

PEINE FORTE ET DURE

August 19, 1692 - September 17, 1692

The hanging of George Burroughs was a mistake. The people started to ask themselves why no one convicted of witchcraft admitted to it. They wondered how these people could come from such pious backgrounds. The reader might well ask, why these people didn't speak out and make their feelings public. The reason was simple: fear. The men in authority had proved that they could convict anyone they wanted to, even if the person was proved innocent. All anybody could do was keep to themselves, at least for now.

The news reached England of the adoption of the old colonial law on witchcraft as a law of the province. England was furious. No new laws could be adopted without their consent. They declared the law illegal and invalid. It would take at least a month for their decision to reach America. In the meantime the trials continued.

On September 9, six more people were brought before the court. Their names were Martha Corey, Mary Easty, Alice Parker, Ann Pudeator, Dorcas Hoar and Mary Bradbury.

Mary Easty was one of Rebecca Nurse's sisters. At her April 22 hearing, her answers had been snappy and to the point. She sounded like she suspected the afflicted girls of being malicious pranksters. The afflicted girls had taken back their accusations after she had been in jail for a while and she was released. Within two days of her release, she was rearrested and sent to Salem on the girls' renewed accusations.

Before her trial, Mary and her sister, Sarah Cloyse, wrote this letter to the Court of Oyer and Terminer:

"The Humble Request of Mary Easty and Sarah Cloyse to the Honored Court humbly showeth that, whereas we two sisters,

Mary Easty and Sarah Cloyse, stand now before the honored Court charged with the suspicion of witchcraft, our humble request is; first that, seeing we are neither able to plead our own cause, nor is council allowed to those in our condition that you who are our judges would please to be of council to us, to direct us wherein we may stand in need.

"Secondly that, whereas we are not conscious to ourselves of any guilt in the least degree of that crime whereof we are now accused (in the presence of the living God we speak it, before whose tribunal we know we shall before long appear), nor of any other scandalous evil or miscarriage inconsistent with Christianity, those who have had the longest and best knowledge of us, being persons of good report, may be asked to testify upon oath what they know concerning each of us; i.e., Mister Capen, the pastor, and those of the town and church of Topsfield, who are ready to say something which we hope may be looked upon as very considerable in this matter, with the seven children of one of us; i.e., Mary Easty. And it may be produced of like nature in reference to the wife of Peter Cloyse, her sister.

"Thirdly that the testimony of the witches, or such as are afflicted as is supposed by witches, may not be called upon to condemn us without other legal evidence concurring.

"We hope the honored Court and jury will be so tender of the lives of such as we are, who have for many years lived under the unblemished reputation of Christianity, as not to condemn them without a fair and equal hearing of what may be said for us as well as against us. And your poor supplicants shall be bound always to pray, etc."

Some time after this request, Sarah Cloyse escaped, saving herself from the fate of her sisters. Mary Easty was sentenced to death. After she received her sentence, she wrote the following petition:

"The Humble Petition of Mary Easty unto his Excellency Sir William Phips, and to the Honored Judge and Bench now sitting in Judicature in Salem, and the Reverend Ministers, humbly showeth that, whereas your poor and humble petitioner, being condemned to die, do humbly beg of you to take it in your judicious and pious consideration that your poor and humble petitioner, knowing my own innocency, blessed be the Lord for it! And seeing plainly the wiles and subtilty of my accusers by myself, cannot but judge charitably of others that are going the same way as myself, if the Lord steps not mightily in.

"I was confined a whole month upon the same account that I am condemned for now, and then cleared by the afflicted persons, as some of your honors know. And in two days time I was cried out upon them, and have been confined, and now am condemned to die. The Lord above knows my innocency then, and likewise does now, as at the great day will be known to men and angels. I petition to Your Honors not for my own life, for I know I must die, and my appointed time is set; but the Lord he knows it is that, if it be possible, no more innocent blood be shed, which undoubtedly cannot be avoided in the way and course you go in.

"I question not but Your Honors do to the utmost of your powers in the discovery and detecting of witchcraft and witches, and would not be guilty of innocent blood for the world. But, by my own innocency, I know you are doing it the wrong way. The Lord in his infinite way direct you in this great work, if it be his blessed will that no more innocent blood be shed!

"I would humbly beg of you that Your Honors would be pleased to examine these afflicted persons carefully, and keep them apart from each other, and do likewise to some of these confessed witches. I am confident that several of them have perjured themselves and others, as will appear, if not in this world, I am sure in the world to come, where I am now going. I question not but that you will see a change in these things. They say, myself and others have made a pact with the Devil, We do not confess to it. I know the Lord knows, as to what is the truth, They lied about me, and so I do not question that they do it to others.

"The Lord above, who is the searcher of all hearts, knows, as I shall answer it at the tribunal seat that I know not the least thing about witchcraft; therefore, I cannot, I dare not, tell lies to my own soul. I beg Your Honors not to deny this my humble petition from a poor, dying, innocent person. And I question not but the Lord will give a blessing to your endeavors."

Martha Corey was the woman that had objected to her husband, Giles, going and listening to the hearings in Salem Village. She had voiced the opinion that she thought they were a bunch of nonsense. Her husband, in a moment of weakness, had helped to accuse her. She was found guilty and sentenced to death. On September 11, Reverend Samuel Parris made the following entry in the church records.

"September 11th, Lord's Day. Sister Martha Corey, taken into the church April 27, 1690, was, after examination upon suspicion of witchcraft, March 27, 1692, committed to prison for that fact, and was condemned to the gallows for the same yesterday; and was this day in public, by a general consent, voted to be excommunicated out of the church, and Lieutenant Nathaniel Putnam and the two deacons chosen to signify her, with the pastor, the mind of the church herein.

"Accordingly, this September 14, 1692, the three aforesaid brethren went with the pastor to her in Salem Prison; whom we found very nasty, justifying herself, and condemning all that had done anything to her just discovery or condemnation. Whereupon, after a little discourse (for her arrogance would not allow much), and after prayer, which she was willing to decline, the dreadful sentence of excommunication was pronounced against her."

Alice Parker had her hearing on May 12. She was the woman that had hassled her husband in Beadle's Tavern, after which one of his drinking buddies was scared by a black hog. As I had mentioned during Alice's hearing, the testimony against Alice and a woman named Mary Parker had become confused with each other. Martha Dutch was one of Alice's accusers. Her deposition is transcribed below:

"The testimony of Martha Dutch aged about 36 years. This deponent testifies and says that about two years ago, the John Jarman, of Salem, was coming home from the sea. I, this deponent and Alice Parker of Salem, as we both stood together, said to her, what a great mercy it was for us to see them coming home well, and through mercy I said my husband had gone and come well many times; and I, this deponent did say unto said Parker that I did hope he would come home well from this voyage also, and said Parker made answer unto me, and said no never more in this world. Which came to pass, as she had told me, for he had died abroad, as I certainly heard."

Martha Dutch's signature appears at the bottom of another piece of evidence written by John Bullock. The date at the bottom is September 7, Alice Parker's trial date. This was one of many documents wrongfully applied at Mary Parker's trial, which took place on September 17.

Alice Parker was sentenced to death.

Ann Pudeator, a widow with five children, had her first hearing on May 12; she was released because of a lack of evidence. On July 2 she was examined again because of a complaint given by Sarah Churchill. Ann said she'd never even seen Sarah before. Constable Joseph Neal had found close to twenty jars partially filled with some kind of grease. When Ann was asked what they were for, she answered that they were for making soap. She was then asked why she didn't pour them all into one jar, since they would fit. She didn't answer the question. The other afflicted girls joined in on her accusation, resulting in her coming to trial. She was found guilty and sentenced to hang.

Ann was well-loved by her family, and her son, Thomas

Greenslit, stayed by her until her execution. She wrote the following petition to the court:

"The Humble Petition of Ann Pudeator unto the Honored Judge and Bench now sitting in Judicature in Salem, humbly showeth that, whereas your poor and humble petitioner, being condemned to die, and knowing in my own conscience, as I shall shortly answer it before the great God of heaven, who is the searcher and knower of all hearts that the evidence of John Best Senior and John Best Junior and Samuel Pickworth, which was given against me in court, were all of them altogether false and untrue, and, besides the abovesaid John Best Senior, has been publicly whipped and recorded for being a liar.

"I would humbly beg of Your Honors to take it into your judicious and pious consideration that my life may not be taken away by such false evidences and witnesses as these; likewise the evidence given in against me by Sarah Churchill and Mary Warren, I am all together ignorant of, and know nothing in the least measure of, nor anything else concerning the crime of witchcraft, for which I am condemned to die, as will be known to men and angels at the great day of judgment.

"Begging and imploring your prayers at the Throne of Grace in my behalf, and your poor and humble petitioner shall forever pray, as she is bound in duty, for Your Honors health and happiness in this life, and eternal felicity in the world to come."

Dorcas Hoar had her first hearing on May 2. She was so outspoken, calling the afflicted liars and gruffly answering the questions that the magistrate had told her not to talk like that. Two of the complaints against her were about a hen of hers that kept going over to a neighbor's yard and damaging his crop. One day the neighbor's son killed it. When they took the dead hen over to Dorcas, she made the comment that it was a sorry week's work. The father of the boys said, "No, it wasn't." A few of the other complaints had to do with her telling people that someone in their family was going to die; in some cases she was right. She dabbled in fortune telling and several witnesses testified to that effect. She was condemned to death.

Mary Bradbury, the wife of Captain Thomas Bradbury, had her first hearing on July 26. Mary was another of those women that had led a spotless life. Several petitions were submitted in her defense. One of them had 115 signatures of the most prominent people in Salisbury. When she was charged she answered the charges in writing.

"The Answer of Mary Bradbury on the charge of Witchcraft or familiarity with the Devil, I do plead not guilty.

"I am wholly innocent of any such wickedness (through the goodness of God that has kept me hitherto), I am the servant of God and have given myself up to him, as my only Lord and Savior; and to the diligent attendance upon him in all his holy ordinances, in utter contempt and defiance of the Devil and all his works as horrid and detestable; and accordingly have endeavored to frame my life and conversation, according to the rules of his holy word, and in that faith and practice, resolve, by the help and assistance of God, to continue to my life's end.

"For the truth of what I say, as to matter of practice, I humbly refer myself, to my brethren and neighbors that know me and unto the searcher of all hearts, for the truth and uprightness of my heart therein; (human frailties and unavoidable infirmities excepted), of which I bitterly complain everyday. Mary Bradbury."

In spite of all the favorable testimony, she was condemned to death.

Giles Corey was the man that had allowed a small squabble with his wife, Martha, to destroy both of their lives. She had been sentenced to death on September 7. The deposition he'd given against Martha must have laid heavily on his conscience. As he sat in prison and heard the sentence that had been passed on her, he must have had a deep feeling of remorse. This fine woman, who had been by his side all these years, was going to pay for a crime that he knew she wasn't guilty of.

He now knew the horrible truth. The other people that he'd watched squirm at the hearings weren't guilty either, and he felt a sense of responsibility for what had happened. Two of his four sons-in-law had testified against Martha. Not once did he object to this. He decided to make his true feelings known and, at the same time, let everyone know exactly how and where he stood. With the cunning that was his stock in trade, he had a will drawn up, or so it has been called. In reality this will was a deed and he had it recorded as such. The deed was written while he was in Ipswich Jail. It read as follows:

"Know ye, &c. that I, Giles Corey, lying under great trouble and affliction, though I am very weak in body, but in perfect memory, knowing not how soon I may depart this life; in consideration of which, and for the fatherly love and affection which I have and do bear unto my beloved son-in-law, William Cleeves, of the town of Beverly, and to my son-in-law, John Moulton, of the town of Salem, as also for diverse and other good causes and considerations given me at the present that are especially moving."

He then listed and conveyed all his property, "lands, meadow, housing, cattle, stock, movables and immovables, money, apparel,... and all other aforesaid premises, with their appurtenances", to the previously mentioned Moulton and Cleeves, "forever, freely and quietly, without any manner of challenge, claim, or demand of me the said Giles Corey, or of any other person or persons whatsoever for me or my name, or by my cause, means, or procurement;" the language he used absolutely conveyed all ownership to his two good son-in-laws, their heirs, executors, administrators, and assignees forever. Giles had it signed by several competent witnesses and had each of them say, in writing that the property was no longer his.

Now that he had given away everything he owned and could never get it back, he embarked on a dark plan. He knew what he had planned for himself would test his courage and his strength. If he came to trial, he would be found guilty, just like all the rest. A guilty verdict would bring with it an issue of Attainder (removal of all civil rights and confiscation of property). If this happened it might invalidate his deed. But, if he was not convicted, or better yet, not tried, the conveyance of his property could not be invalidated. He decided he would not be tried.

When he was summoned before the court, on September 17, they read the charges against him. When it came time to enter his plea of guilty or not guilty, he just stood there. Three times he was called to the bench and each time he refused to answer. In his heart he knew that if he had pleaded not guilty, he would have been condoning the legitimacy of the court to hear his case - a case he knew he couldn't have won because Justice was completely blind and deaf at that time.

The court was at a loss for what to do. They had never had a person refuse to plead before. They probably read the charges and said aloud that he refused to answer. After the third try, the sentence of peine forte et dure, was pronounced. This punishment had an exact procedure, as prescribed by English law. How strictly it was adhered to by the Salem Jail will remain a secret locked within its walls. Giles was dragged from the court and thrown into the darkest dungeon. On September 17, Giles Corey's sentence was started. For the reader's benefit, I will describe the law of peine forte et dure and its legend. Somewhere between these two is what really happened.

Peine forte et dure was a law developed in medieval times to force a man that stood mute at his trial to speak his plea. The man was taken to the worst cell in the dungeons of the prison. His clothes were taken off and he was made to lay down with his back to the floor. Iron weights were placed on his body. The weight of them was just short of crushing him. On the first day he was given three pieces of the worst moldy bread to eat. The next day he was given three sips of water from the stagnant puddle nearest the jail cell. This procedure was repeated until the man either pleaded or died.

Now the way it supposedly happened in Salem. Tradition says that on September 17 Giles Corey was taken to an open field near the jail. He was laid on the ground and rocks were piled on top of him. He supposedly asked for more rocks, explaining that he wasn't going to give in so they might as well get it over with. His request was refused. Giles, an old man of eighty-one years, took this slow, crushing death for two days. As the weight crushed the life out of him, his tongue came out of his mouth. An official, standing nearby, pushed it back in with his cane.

The Reverend Noyes held a special week-day service. In the church log he wrote the following, "September 18, Giles Corey was excommunicated: the cause of it was that he being accused and indicted for the sin of witchcraft, he refused to plead, and so incurred the sentence of peine forte et dure; being undoubtedly either guilty of the sin of witchcraft, or of throwing himself upon sudden and certain death, if he were otherwise innocent."

Judge Samuel Sewall wrote in his diary, "Monday, September 19, 1692. About noon, at Salem, Giles Corey was pressed to death for standing mute; much pains was used with him two days, one after another, by the Court and Captain Gardner of Nantucket who had been of his acquaintance: But all in vain."

Giles has the dubious distinction of being the only person in America to have suffered this kind of punishment.

Giles Corey's death had caused considerable commotion among the people. For the first time they were speaking out loud about the injustices of the witch trials. This was bad for business, so the next day, September 20, Judge Samuel Sewall received a letter from Thomas Putnam.

"Last night, my daughter Ann was grievously tormented by witches, threatening that she should be pressed to death before Giles Corey; but, through the goodness of a gracious God, she had at last a little respite. Whereupon there appeared unto her (she said), a man in a bed sheet, who told her that Giles Corey had murdered him by pressing him to death with his feet; but that the Devil there appeared unto him, and covenanted with him, and promised him that he should not be hanged.

"The Apparition said God hardened his heart that he should not listen to the advise of the Court, and so die an easy death; because, as it said, it must be done to him as he has done unto me. The apparition also said that Giles Corey was carried to the

Court for this, and that the jury had found the murderer; and that her father knew the man, and the thing was done before she was born."

This "vision", was deemed by Cotton Mather as proof positive of Ann's supernatural abilities. He felt that the only way she could know about the man Giles Corey had beaten to death eighteen years ago, was by being able to talk to his ghost. Cotton Mather stressed the fact that Ann Putnam hadn't even been born when the incident occurred. He went on to say that everyone had forgotten the incident, so she couldn't possibly have heard it from someone alive. The people did remember, of course, and this story placated them for a little while. Remembering the murder took some of the sympathy away from Giles' brutal death.

Judge Samuel Sewall's entry in his diary read, "September 20. Now I hear from Salem that about eighteen years ago, he was suspected to have stamped and pressed a man to death, but was cleared. Twas not remembered till Anne Putnam was told of it by said Corey's specter the Sabbath day, night before execution."

Notice that Judge Samuel Sewall misread the letter and thought that it had been Giles Corey's specter that Ann had claimed to have seen.

Aside from Giles Corey, eight other people were brought to trial on September 17: Margaret Scott, Wilmott Reed, Samuel Wardwell, Mary Parker, Abigail Faulkner, Mary Lacy Senior, Ann Foster and Abigail Hobbs.

Mary Parker, a widow, was examined on September 2 and bound over for trial. A considerable amount of evidence has been attributed to her case that doesn't belong to her. It appears that all of the testimony dated September 7, 1692, actually belonged to Alice Parker, whose trial was in progress on that date. Both women lived in the town of Andover, and had husbands by the name of John (Mary's husband had died). Their husbands were both mariners. The problem arose because the people writing the depositions left out the first name of the defendant. If this was true, Mary was condemned for her last name. She was sentenced to death.

Six weeks after her execution, Mary's sons petitioned the governing body. The contents of this document should prove of interest to the reader.

"To his Excellency the Governor, and Council and Representatives, now sitting in Boston, the humble Petition of John Parker and Joseph Parker of Andover showeth that whereas our mother Mary Parker of Andover, was apprehended upon suspicion of witchcraft, and being brought to trial at Salem court, was condemned. Since her death the sheriff (George Corwin) of Essex, sent an officer to seize on her estate. The said officer required us in their majesties name to give him an account of our mother's estate, pretending that it was forfeited to the King. We told him that our mother left no estate, (which we are able to prove) notwithstanding which, he seized upon our cattle, corn and hay, to a considerable value; and ordered us to go to Salem and make an agreement with the sheriff, otherwise the estate would be put up for sale.

"We, not knowing what advantage the law might give him against us, and fearing we should sustain greater damage by the loss of our estate, went to the sheriff accordingly, who told us he might take away that which was seized, if he pleased, but was willing to do us a kindness by giving us an opportunity to redeem it. He at first demanded ten pounds from us, but at length was willing to take six pounds, which he has obliged us, by bill, to pay him within a month.

"Now, if our mother had left any estate, we know not of any law in this province, by which it should be forfeited upon her condemnation; much less can we understand that there is any justice or reason, for the sheriff to seize upon our estate. And though it is true our own act has obliged us to pay him a sum of money, yet we declare that we were drawn to it partly by the officer's great pretenses of law for what he did, and partly to prevent the loss of our estate, which we feared would be immediately sold.

"Now we humbly pray this Honored Court to consider our case, and if it be judged that so much money ought not to have been demanded of us, upon the aforementioned account; we pray that we may be discharged from that obligation, which the sheriff, taking advantage of our ignorance, has brought us under. And your petitioners as in duty bound shall ever pray, etc."

It is not known if this petition was granted. This is another one of several documents alluding to Sheriff George Corwin's abuses of the law for his own personal gain.

CHAPTER XII

THE DAWN OF REASON

September 17, 1692 - December 23, 1692

The next person to be brought before the bench was Margaret Scott. All that remains of her history are two depositions. Both documents are dated September 15 and appear on the same page in the county records. The first one was made by Francis Wycom. It stated that the specter of Margaret Scott appeared and tormented her up until the time of Margaret's hearing on August 5. The second deposition was written by Phillip and Sarah Nelson. It is reprinted below.

"--also Phillip Nelson and Sarah his wife do testify and say that for two or three years before the said Robert Shilloto died, we have often heard him complaining of Margaret Scott for hurting of him and often said that she was a witch and so he continued complaining of Margaret Scott saying he should never be well as long as Margaret Scott lived and so he complained of Margaret Scott: at times until he died.

"Phillip Nelson and Sarah his wife affirmed: upon their oath to the grand inquest that the above written evidence: is the truth."

You can be sure the afflicted girls put on their usual display when she came in. Obviously they didn't even know her by their lack of depositions. Margaret was found guilty and sentenced to hang.

Wilmott "Mammy" Reed's hearing had taken place on May 31. The accusations surrounding her trial were based on an incident that had happened five years earlier. A Miss Sims had some linen turn up missing. She suspected Martha Laurence, a girl living with Wilmott Reed. Miss Sims came over to Wilmott's house with another woman by the name of Charity Pitman and tried to get her linen back. Wilmott Reed refused to let her enter. Miss Sims threatened to complain to the magistrate. Wilmott told her if she did that, she hoped the woman would have a constipation problem. Miss Sims did come down with constipation shortly afterwards. Her bowel problem lasted for several months.

Wilmott Reed was condemned to death.

Samuel Wardwell had originally been examined on September 1. At the hearing he confessed that he was a witch, naming some other innocent people in the process. On September 14 he recanted, saying that the confession was spoken by him but that he had perjured himself. He said that it was his only lie and he knew that he would die for it, whether he admitted it or not.

Samuel Wardwell was right; he was condemned to death.

Abigail Faulkner was the daughter of Reverend Francis Dane of Andover. She had been examined on August 11. At her hearing Magistrate Hathorne asked her, "Don't you see these girls afflictions?" Her unusual answer was, "Yes, but it is the Devil doing it in my shape." Ann Putnam accused Abigail of having pulled her off her horse a few days earlier. She denied any guilt but was sent to jail.

On August 30, Abigail was brought before the bench again. Meanwhile, six people had been executed for witchcraft. At this hearing she had expressed her indignation at the way the afflicted children were acting and was very much annoyed at them "for bringing her kindred out, and she wished them ill: and her spirit being raised, she did pinch her hands together, and she knew not but that the Devil might take that advantage; but it was the Devil and not she that afflicted them." This was the only thing she would say and the magistrates were confused as to whether it was a confession or not. At her trial on September 17, the verdict was handed down. Being one of the few surviving documents of this type, it is printed below:

"At the Court of Oyer and Terminer holding at Salem by adjournment, September 1692"

"Abigail Faulkner of Andover, indicted and arraigned for the crime of felony by witchcraft, committed on the bodies of Martha Sprague, evidences being called and sworn in open court, matter of fact committed the jury.

"The jury find Abigail Faulkner wife of Francis Faulkner of Andover, guilty of the felony by witchcraft committed on the body of Martha Sprague, also on the body of Sarah Phelps-

"Sentence of death passed on Abigail Faulkner"

Rebecca Eames confessed that she was a witch at her hearing on August 19 and again on August 31. At her trial, she was condemned to death.

Mary Lacy Senior confessed that she was a witch on July 21.

She implicated her mother, Ann Foster, by accusing her of riding on a pole with her and Martha Carrier to a meeting in Salem Village. Because of this testimony, Mary Lacy Junior would be arrested and accused of witchcraft. Mary Lacy Senior was found guilty and sentenced to death.

Ann Foster, Mary Lacy Senior's mother, was of course sentenced on her daughter's testimony to death.

Abigail Hobbs was the insane young woman that had baptized her mother in front of company. Her hearing was held on April 19, where she admitted that she was a witch. Since that time, she had accused several others of the same crime. She was condemned to death.

The sentence of death was to be carried out on September 22. Of the sixteen people brought before the bench in September for witchcraft, one had been crushed (Giles Corey) and fifteen were sentenced to death. Only eight of them would make the painful journey. Seven of them would escape the gallows. One of these women used the excuse of pregnancy to get a reprieve. That may have been the Reverend Francis Dane's daughter, Abigail Faulkner.

Abigail Hobbs, Rebecca Eames, and Mary Lacy Senior were useful to the prosecutors as witnesses and the sentence of death kept them in control.

On December 5, Rebecca Eames wrote a petition to Governor William Phips:

"The humble Petition of Rebecca Eames unto his Excellency Sir William Phips Knight and Governor of their Majesties Dominions in America humbly showeth,

"That whereas your poor and humble petitioner having been here closely confined in Salem prison, near four months, and likewise condemned to die for the crime of witchcraft, which the Lord above knows I am altogether innocent of, as will appear at the great day of judgment, having had no evidence against me, but the specter evidences and my own confession, which the Lord above knows was altogether false and untrue, I being hurried out of my senses by the afflicted persons, Abigail Hobbs and Mary Lacy, who, both of them, cried out against me, charging me with witchcraft for four days, mocking me and spitting in my face, saying they knew me to be an old witch and if I would not confess it, I should very speedily be hanged, for there was some such that had gone before me and I should follow them, which was the occasion, with my own wicked heart, of my saying what I did say.

"And the reason of my standing to my confession at my trial was that I knew not one word that I said when I was upon my trial, nor what the honored magistrate said to me, but only the name of Queen Mary; but may it please your Excellency: When Mister Mather (Increase) and Mister Brattle (Thomas) were here in Salem, they took back what they before had said against me, and do still admit and say, what they had said against me, was nothing but the Devil's delusions and they knew nothing in the least measure of any witchcraft by me. Your poor and humble petitioner do beg and implore of your Excellency, to take it into your pious heart and judicious consideration, to grant me a pardon of my life, not deserving death by man for witchcraft or any other sin that my innocent blood may not be shed.

"And your poor and humble petitioner shall pray, as she is bound in duty for your health and happiness in this life and eternal felicity in the world to come. So prays your poor and humble petitioner."

Out of desperation, Ann Foster confessed that she was a witch, saving herself from the gallows. Shortly after her confession, she died from the deplorable prison conditions. Her son, Abraham, had to pay two pounds and ten shillings to retrieve her body for burial.

John Hale, Nicholas Noyes, Daniel Epes, and John Emerson Junior wrote the following petition and submitted it to the court on September 21:

"To his Excellency Sir William Phips, Governor of the Province of the Massachusetts Colony in New England or in his absence to the Honorable William Stoughton Esquire, Lieutenant Governor.

"The petition of the subscribers humbly shows that it has pleased the Lord, we hope, in mercy to the soul of Dorcas Hoar, of Beverly, to open her heart, out of distress of conscience, as she professes, to confess herself guilty of the heinous crime of witchcraft for which she is condemned, and how and when she was taken in the snare of the Devil, and that she signed his book with the forefinger of her right hand &c.

"Also she gives account of some other persons that she has known, to be guilty of the same crime.

"And being in great distress of conscience, earnestly craves a little longer time of life, to realize and perfect her repentance, for the salvation of her soul.

"These are therefore humbly to petition in her behalf that there may be granted her one month's time or more to prepare her for death and eternity, unless by her relapse or afflicting of others, she shall give grounds to hasten her execution. And this we conceive if the Lord sanctify, it may tend to save a soul, and to give opportunity for her making some discovery of these mysteries of iniquity, and be providential to the encouraging of others to confess and give glory to God."

In the blank space below the petition, Judge Bartholomew Gedney wrote:

"Having heard and taken the confession of Dorcas Hoar, do consent that her execution be delayed until further notice."

The signature of Nicholas Noyes was probably mandatory to assure a person's sentence being changed. The most interesting thing about this document is the Reverend Hale's signature. He was already on his way back to sanity when it was written. We will discuss more of this later.

Abigail Faulkner, as mentioned earlier, was the daughter of the Reverend Francis Dane. The Reverend Francis Dane of Andover had locally spoken out against the witchcraft trials. His signature was on the petitions presented to the court for some of the accused. The afflicted children tried to get at him without making the mistake of accusing him directly. Abigail Faulkner was only one of several of his relatives accused by them. Another of his daughters, Elizabeth Johnson, and her daughter, Elizabeth Johnson Junior, were both imprisoned for trial. Several of his grandchildren, family servants and his daughter-in-law were also imprisoned. There is some evidence that Elizabeth Howe, executed on July 19, was the wife of his nephew.

For some unknown reason, Governor William Phips ordered a reprieve for Abigail Faulkner. It is believed that this was the only time a special pardon was granted during the proceedings.

Mary Bradbury was the seventh person that escaped the hangman. She was the woman who had all those depositions submitted on her behalf. I found no indication that she confessed to witchcraft. One possibility was that the people were becoming unsettled about the whole affair and the prosecutors felt it best not to execute a person with such overwhelming support. Whatever the reason, she would never hang. Shortly after her conviction, she was broken out of prison by some of her friends.

On September 22, Martha Corey, Mary Easty, Alice Parker, Mary Parker, Ann Pudeator, Margaret Scott, Wilmott "Mammy" Reed, and Samuel Wardwell were put in a wooden cart and taken on their long trek through the town of Salem to Gallows Hill. There is no information available concerning Alice Parker, Mary Parker, Margaret Scott, Ann Pudeator or Wilmott Reed's last moments. We can assume that they died with the piety of the previous victims since none of the prosecutors said anything detrimental about them in their moment of death.

Calef says that, "Martha Corey, protesting her innocence,

concluded her life with an eminent prayer upon the ladder."

That morning Mary Easty met with her family in prison for the last time. The people who had overheard what she said to them reported that she was "as serious, religious, distinct, and affectionate as could well be expressed, drawing tears from the eyes of almost all those present." She carried herself with solemnity to the place of her execution and died with unnerving dignity.

Samuel Wardwell was the man who had originally confessed and then, stricken by his conscience, had the courage to recant it. While he was speaking to the people from the ladder, a puff of smoke from the executioner's pipe hit him in the face, causing him to interrupt his speech. His accusers said that the Devil was hindering him with smoke. When he had finished declaring his innocence, he said a prayer and died.

The court recessed until the first Tuesday in November; undoubtedly they planned to meet each month to send more victims to the hangman. Unknown to them, the court of Oyer and Terminer had tried its last witchcraft case. So many things happened between September 22 and the middle of October that chronology is a jumbled mess. The different events have been grouped separately for the reader to follow easily. Added together, they produced the fastest change of an historical path ever recorded. The underground movement had been built to tremendous proportions. Public outcry began to surface everywhere. The afflicted girls had become overconfident in their accusations. Eventually they accused Governor Phips' wife because she had given a prisoner freedom in her husband's name while he was off to war. They accused a member of Increase Mather's family because he didn't go along with their type of evidence. Even Judge Jonathan Corwin's mother-in-law was accused because he didn't seem to have his heart in the proceedings.

In a public speech at Cambridge on October 3, Increase Mather repeated his views on spectral evidence. He told the audience of clergymen that it was better to let ten witches go than to condemn one innocent person. Increase Mather's preliminary books had achieved wide circulation by October 11, showing those in authority what the clergy's feelings on spectral evidence really were. Their opinions, no longer private, spread like wild fire.

A wealthy merchant by the name of Thomas Brattle wrote a letter on October 8. Although it didn't get published, it was widely circulated. It was addressed to an unknown minister in response to some questions regarding the witch trials. The letter is quite lengthy. For those readers who would like to read it, you will find it in *Narratives of the Witchcraft Cases 1648-1706*, by G. L. Burr,

Barnes and Noble, 1946.

The general gist of the letter was that the afflicted children would have been cured by anyone who put the right kind of touch to them. He made no bones about the judges illogical theories of the accused's sight afflicting the children but not afflicting the judges. He continued by pointing out the lack of a warrant for Margaret Thatcher, Judge Corwin's mother-in-law who had been accused often; and the exceptional treatment of Hezekiah Usher, who was held in a plush home for two weeks and allowed to escape without anyone noticing that he was gone. Meanwhile others accused of the same crime were thrown into dungeons and denied bail. He wondered how people like Mister English or Mister Alden could have escaped with everyone knowing where they were hiding, and yet no arrest warrants were issued nor any efforts made to bring them back.

Thomas Brattle's letter was an eye opener in its clean, precise logic and it would continue to gain fame in the years to come.

The town of Andover had several citizens who, as soon as they heard the beginning public outcry, launched massive lawsuits for slander against the accusers. A rich gentleman in Boston sent some men with arrest warrants to Andover. Their job was to arrest those that had accused the gentleman of witchcraft and press a thousand pound defamation lawsuit against each and every one of his accusers. This tactic scared people into retracting their testimony.

Governor Phips sent a letter to William Blathwayt, Clerk of the Privy Council in Great Britain, on October 12:

"When I first arrived I found this province miserably harassed with a most horrible witchcraft or possession of devils, which had broken in on several towns, some scores (one score equals twenty) of poor people were taken with preternatural torments, some scalded with brimstone, some had pins stuck in their flesh, others hurried into the fire and water and some dragged out of their houses and carried over the tops of trees and hills for many miles together; it has been represented to me much like that of Sweden about thirty years ago, and there were many committed to prison upon suspicion of witchcraft before my arrival.

"The loud cries and clamors of the friends of the afflicted people, with the advise of the Deputy Governor and many others, prevailed with me to give a commission of Oyer and Terminer for discovering what witchcraft might be at the bottom, or whether it were not a possession.

"The chief judge in this commission was the Deputy Governor and the rest were persons of the best prudence and figure that could then be pitched upon.

"When the Court came to sit at Salem, in the County of Essex, they convicted more then twenty persons of being guilty of witchcraft, some of the convicted were such as confessed their guilt, the Court as I understand began their proceedings with the accusations of the afflicted and then went upon other human evidences to strengthen that.

"I was almost the whole time of the proceeding abroad in the service of Their Majesties, in the eastern part of the county and depended upon the judgment of the Court, as to a right method of proceeding in cases of witchcraft, but when I came home I found many persons in a strange ferment of dissatisfaction, which was increased by some hot spirits that blew up the flame, but on inquiring into the matter; I found that the Devil had taken upon him the name and shape of several persons who were doubtless innocent and to my certain knowledge of good reputation, for which cause I have now forbidden the committing of any more that shall be accused without unavoidable necessity, and those that have been committed I would shelter from any proceedings against them, wherein there may be the least suspicion of any wrong to be done unto the innocent.

"I would also wait for any particular directions or commands, if their Majesties please to give me any, for the fuller ordering of this perplexed affair.

"I have also put a stop to the printing of any discourses one way or other that may increase the disputes of people upon this occasion, because I saw a likelihood of kindling an inextinguishable flame, if I should admit any public and open contests and I have grieved to see that some, who should have done their Majesties and this Province better service, have so far taken council of passion as to desire the precipitancy of these matters, these things have been improved by some to give me many interruptions in their Majesties service and in truth none of my vexations have been greater than this, than that their Majesties service has been hereby unhappily clogged, and the persons who have made so ill improvement of these matters here are seeking to turn it all upon me, but I hereby declare that as soon as I came from fighting against their Majesties enemies and understood what danger some of their innocent subjects might be exposed to, if the evidence of the afflicted persons only did prevail either to the committing or trying any of them, I did before any application was made unto me about it put a stop to the proceedings of the Court and they are now stopped till their Majesties pleasure be known.

"Sir, I beg pardon for giving you all this trouble, the reason is, because I know my enemies are seeking to turn it all upon me and I take this liberty, because I depend upon your friendship, and desire you will please to give a true understanding of the matter, if anything of this kind be urged or made use of against me. Because the justness of my proceeding herein will be a sufficient defense. Sir I am with all imaginable respect your most humble servant William Phips."

William Blathwayt, wrote this memorandum on the bottom:

"That my Lord President be pleased to acquaint his Majesty in Council, with the account received from New England from Sir William Phips the Governor there, touching proceedings against several persons for witchcraft as appears by the Governor's letter concerning those matters."

After Governor Phips wrote this letter, he commanded that no more trials be held until he received guidance from England. On October 29, he ordered the Court of Oyer and Terminer dissolved.

Samuel Sewall wrote, "October 29, Mister Russell asked whether the Court of Oyer and Terminer should sit, expressing some fear of inconvenience by it's fall. Governor said it must fall."

The accusation that broke the spell was the one against Reverend John Hale's wife on November 14. Her virtues were well known and her reputation was engraved in the minds of the people. When the girls accused her, the whole community knew they were liars and no one believed anything they had to say afterwards.

On November 25, the General Court created the Superior Court of Judicature to hear the rest of the witch cases. The judges were Lieutenant Governor William Stoughton, who was to be the Chief Justice, Thomas Danforth, Samuel Sewall, John Richards, and Wait Still Winthrop, the associate justices.

On December 14, the General Court passed a bill on the punishment for witchcraft.

"A Bill Against Conjuration, Witchcraft, and Dealing with Evil and Wicked Spirits (December 1692)"

For more particular direction in the execution of the law against witchcraft.

"-Be it enacted by the Governor's Council and Representatives in General Court assembled and by the authority of the same that if any person or persons shall use, practice or exercise any invocation or conjuration of any evil or wicked spirit, or shall consult, covenant with, entertain, employ, feed or reward any evil and wicked spirit to or for any intent or purpose. Or take up any dead man, woman or child, out of his, her or their grave, or any other place where the dead body rests, or the skin, bone or any other part of any dead person, to be employed or used in any manner of witchcraft, sorcery, charm or enchantment, or shall use, practice or exercise any witchcraft, enchantment, charm or sorcery, whereby any person shall be killed, destroyed, wasted, consumed, pined or lamed in his or her body, or any part thereof.

"That, then every such offender or offenders, their aiders, abetters and counselors being of any the said offenses, duly and lawfully convicted and attained, shall suffer pains of death as a felon or felons. And further to the intent of all manner and practice, use or exercise of witchcraft or enchantment, charm or sorcery, should be henceforth utterly avoided, abolished or taken away.

"Be it enacted by the authority aforesaid that if any person or persons shall take upon him or them by witchcraft, enchantment charm or sorcery, to tell or declare in what place any treasure of gold or silver should or might be found or hid in the earth or other secret places or where goods or things, lost or stolen, should be found or become; or to the intent to provoke any person to unlawful love, or whereby any cattle or goods of any person shall be destroyed, wasted or impaired; or to hurt or destroy any person in his or her body, although the same be not effected and done.

"That, then all and every such person and persons so offending, and being thereof lawfully convicted, shall, for the said offenses, suffer imprisonment by the space of one whole year, without bail or reprieve, and once every quarter of the said year, shall in some shire town, stand openly, by the pillory by the space of six hours, and there shall openly confess his or her error and offense, which said offense shall be written in capitol letters and placed upon the breast of said offender.

"And if any person or persons, being once convicted of the same offense, and shall again commit the like offense, and being of any of the said offenses the second time, lawfully and duly, convicted and attained, as is aforesaid, shall suffer pains of death as a felon or felons.

"Read several times in Council, voted, ordered to be engrossed and passed in to an act, die predict. And is consented unto, William Phips."

On December 23, a warrant for jurors was issued.

CHAPTER XIII

RECOMPENSE

January 2, 1693 - August 28, 1957

Beginning January 3, 1693, fifty-two people were brought to trial on the charge of witchcraft. When the trials were over, three of the people were condemned to death. Judge William Stoughton hurriedly signed their death warrants. Then he signed the death warrants for five of the convicted prisoners from the September trials.

The Attorney General brought this to the attention of Governor Phips, telling him that the convicted people had been condemned by the same evidence as the other forty-nine people had been acquitted. Angry, Governor Phips ordered the release of the eight condemned individuals. Lieutenant Governor William Stoughton resigned from the court. From then on, no more convictions were made.

On February 21, Governor Phips wrote a letter to the Earl of Nottingham:

"May it please your Lordship. By the Captain of the Samuel and Henry, I gave an account that, at my arrival here, I found prisons full of people committed upon suspicion of witchcraft, and that continual complaints were made to me that many persons were grievously tormented by witches, and that they cried out upon several persons by name, as the cause of their torments.

"The number of these complaints increasing every day, by advise of the Lieutenant Governor and the Council, I gave a commission of Oyer and Terminer to try the suspected witches and at that time, the generality of the people represented to me, as real witchcraft and gave very strange instances of the same.

"The head of the commission was the Lieutenant Governor and the rest, persons of the best prudence and figure that could be found, and I depended upon the Court for a correct method of

137

proceeding in the witchcraft cases.

"At that time I went to command the army at the eastern part of the Province, for the French and Indians had made an attack upon some of our frontier towns. I continued there for some time, but when I returned, I found the people much dissatisfied at the proceedings of the Court, for about twenty persons were condemned and executed, of which number, some were thought by many persons to be innocent.

"The Court still proceeded in the same method of trying them, which was by the evidence of the afflicted persons, who, when they were brought into the Court, as soon as the suspected witches looked upon them, instantly fell to the ground, in strange agonies and grievous torments, but when touched by them, upon the arm or some other part of their flesh, they immediately revived and came to themselves, upon which, they made oath that the prisoner at the bar, did afflict them and that they saw their shape or specter, come from their bodies, which put them to such pains and torments.

"When I inquired into the matter I was informed, by the judges that they began with this, but had human testimony against such as were condemned and undoubted proof of their being witches, but at length I found that the Devil did take upon him the shape of innocent persons and some were accused, of whose innocency I was well assured and many considerable persons, of blameless lives and conversation, were cried out upon as witches and wizards.

"The Lieutenant Governor, notwithstanding, persisted vigorously in the same method, to the great dissatisfaction and disturbance of the people, until I put an end to the Court and stopped the proceedings, which I did because I saw many innocent persons might otherwise perish and, at the same time, I thought it my duty to give an account thereof that their Majesties pleasure might be signified, hoping that, for the better ordering thereof, the judges learned of the law in England, might give such rules and directions, as have been practiced in England, for proceedings in so difficult and so nice a point.

"When I put an end to the Court there were at least fifty persons, in prison, in great misery, by reason of the extreme cold and their poverty, most of them having only spectral evidence against them, and their mittimuses being defective, I caused some of them to be let out upon bail and put the judges upon considering of a way to relieve others, and prevent them from perishing in prison, upon which, some of them, were convinced and acknowledged that their former proceedings were too violent and not grounded upon a right foundation, but that if they might sit again, they would proceed after another method, and whereas Mister Increase Mather and several other divines did give it as their judgment that the Devil might afflict in the shape of an innocent person and that the look and touch of the suspected persons, was not sufficient proof against them, these things had not the same stress laid upon them as before, and upon this consideration I permitted a special Superior Court, to be held at Salem, in the County of Essex, on the third day of January, the Lieutenant Governor being Chief Judge.

"Their method being changed, all that were brought to trial, totaling fifty-two, were cleared except for three, and I was informed by the King's Attorney General that some of the cleared and the condemned were under the same circumstances, or that there was the same reason to clear the three condemned, as the rest, according to his judgment. The Lieutenant Governor, signed a warrant for their speedy execution and also of five others, who were condemned at the former Court of Oyer and Terminer, but considering how the matter had been managed, I sent a reprieve, whereby the execution was stopped, until their Majesties' pleasure be signified and declared.

"The Lieutenant Governor, upon this occasion, was enraged and filled with passionate anger and refused to sit upon the bench in a Superior Court, then held in Charles Town, and indeed has, from the beginning, hurried on these matters with great precipitancy, and by his warrant, has caused the estates, goods and chattels, of the executed, to be seized and disposed of, without my knowledge or consent.

"The stop, put to the first method of proceedings, has dissipated the black cloud that threatened this Province with destruction; for whereas this delusion of the Devil did spread and its dismal effects, touched the lives and estates of many of their Majesties' subjects and the reputation of some of the principal persons here, and indeed unhappily, clogged and interrupted their Majesties' affairs, which have been a great vexation to me, I have no new complaints, but peoples' minds, before divided and distracted, by differing opinions concerning this matter, are now well composed."

Obviously, by the tone of this and his previous letter, the Governor was afraid that the whole thing was going to be blamed on him.

On March 10, Lydia Dustin died in prison. She had been acquitted on January 31, but was unable to pay her prison charges.

In May, 1693, Governor Phips discharged all remaining prisoners by proclamation. The number of people set free was said to have been 150, the largest number of prisoners ever released at one time in New England. There was one catch: no one could leave until they had paid their prison charges, which included jailer's fees, court costs, room and board. Many of the people had become completely impoverished and couldn't pay for freedom.

Margaret Jacobs was one of the unfortunate ones. She was the daughter of George Jacobs Junior, the man who had run away leaving his mentally ill wife and small children to fend for themselves. When Margaret and her mother were arrested, the children had been abandoned by the authorities and eventually taken in by charitable neighbors. When her grandfather was executed, his property was seized by the sheriff. Margaret's house had been completely emptied of its contents, left open and deserted. She was kept in prison for a considerable time. Finally a fisherman by the name of Gammon, hearing of her ordeal, raised the money to pay for her release. It took the Jacobs' family several years to repay the kind and sympathetic stranger.

Tituba, the woman from the West Indies who helped to start the hysteria, was promised by Parris that she would be freed for her cooperative testimony. He didn't follow through with his promise. She recanted her story, saying that Samuel Parris had beaten her into confessing herself a witch. She said that everything she'd confessed or said to accuse others was a direct result of those beatings. In May of 1693, Tituba was sold to someone else; she would never see the Parris family again.

Several of the prominent players in this tragedy died shortly afterwards. Marshal Herrick died in 1695 at the age of thirty-seven; he was the man responsible for the arrests, imprisonment and examinations of the early victims. His acts concerning the prisoners had stirred up a lot of resentment. When George Corwin became sheriff, he inherited this resentment. Herrick stayed on as deputy. On December 8, 1692, Herrick petitioned the court, complaining that his time had been so taken up by arresting and transporting people from prison to prison that his family life had suffered and he'd lost his house. He begged them for recompense, "for I have been bred a gentleman, and not much use to work, and am become despicable in these hard times." His petition concluded with the statement that, if the court provided for him and his family, he would accept any job they gave him no matter how dangerous.

Sheriff George Corwin died in 1697 at the age of thirty-one. Phillip English, who had lost a considerable amount of money by way of Corwin's collecting practices, put a lean on Corwin's corpse. The body was deposited on George Corwin's front lawn until his executors paid Phillip English sixty pounds and three shillings, almost all that was left of the estate.

Thomas Putnam and his wife, Ann, died within fifteen days of each other. Thomas died on May 24, 1699, at the age of forty-seven, and Ann died on June 8 at the age of thirty-eight. Their daughter, Ann Putnam Junior, had been the leading instigator of the trials. There is some indication that the Putnams regretted their participation in the affair. If this was so, they must have had a terrible burden to bear.

Samuel Parris was finally ousted by the people of Salem Village in 1697. Because of his continuous refusal to take advice, the ministry lost all sympathy for him. At one point they had offered him a good job if he would end his squabble with the village and leave gracefully. He refused so when he was finally ousted, the best jobs he could get were in impoverished conditions. His reputation followed him everywhere he went. Never again would he be in a position like the one he had attained at Salem Village. Little Elizabeth married Benjamin Barnes of Concord in 1710. Samuel Parris died in Sudbury on February 27, 1720.

The Reverend Joseph Green was Parris's successor in Salem Village. His ministry brought an end to the nearly thirty years of strife the village had been under since it was first founded. After his ordination on November 10, 1698, Reverend Green set upon a path that would bring the village together, in forgiveness and atonement. The following are some excerpts from the church records, as transcribed in Charles Upham's supplement to his book, *Salem Witchcraft*. They tell in the minister's own words how reconciliation was accomplished.

"November 28, 1698, being spent in holy exercise (in order to our preparation for the Sacrament for the Lord's Supper), at John Putnam Junior's. After the exercise, I desired the church to manifest, by the usual sign, that they were so cordially satisfied with their brethren, Thomas Wilkins, Thomas Tarbell and Samuel Nurse. That they were heartily desirous that they would join with us in all ordinances. That so we might all live lovingly together. This they consented unto, and none made any objection, but voted it by lifting up their hands. And further that whatsoever articles they had drawn up against these brethren, formerly, they now look upon them as nothing, but let them fall to the ground, being willing that they should be buried forever.

"February 5, 1699. This day, also John Tarbell and his wife, and Thomas Wilkins and his wife, and Samuel Nurse's wife, joined with us in the Lord's Supper; which is a matter of thankfulness, seeing they have for a long time been so offended as that they could not comfortably join with us.

"1702. In December, the pastor spoke at the church, on the Sabbath, as follows: 'Brethren, I find in your church book a record of Martha Corey's being excommunicated for witchcraft; and, the generality of the land being sensible of the errors that prevailed in that day, some of her friends have moved me several times to propose to the church whether it be not our duty to recall that sentence, so that it may not stand against her for all generations; and I myself being a stranger to her, and being ignorant of what was alleged against her, I shall now only leave it to your consideration, and shall determine the matter by a vote the next convenient opportunity.'

"February 14, 1703. The major part of the brethren consented to the following: 'Whereas this church passed a vote, September 11, 1692, for the excommunication of Martha Corey, and that sentence was pronounced against her September 14 by Mister Samuel Parris, formerly the pastor of this church; she being, before her excommunication, condemned, and afterwards executed, for supposed witchcraft; and there being a record of this in our church book, page twelve, we being moved hereunto, do freely consent and heartily desire that the same sentence may be revoked, and that it may stand no longer against her; for we are, through God's mercy to us, convinced that we were at that dark day under the power of those errors which then prevailed in the land; and we are sensible that we had not sufficient grounds to think her guilty of that crime for which she was condemned and executed; and that her excommunication was not according to the mind of God, and therefore we desire that this may be entered in our church book, to take off that odium that is cast on her name, and that so God may forgive our sin, and may be atoned for the land; and we humbly pray that God will not leave us any more to such errors and sins, but will teach and enable us always to do that which is right in his sight.'

"There was a major part voted and six or seven dissented. Joseph Green, Pastor."

This forward approach by Reverend Green was taken almost ten years before sentiment was to turn in favor of such things. In March of 1712, the First Church of Salem would take similar actions in the cases of Rebecca Nurse and Giles Corey.

From the latter half of 1692 onward, several petitions were submitted to the court for restitution. The victims had lost, in most cases, all of their assets. The process was so lengthy that Phillip

English's claim didn't see final action until November 1718, at which time he was awarded two hundred pounds for his fifteen hundred pound loss. The last petition of record was from the heirs of George Burroughs; it was acted upon March 28, 1750.

The brand of witchcraft hung as a heavy burden around the necks of the accused and their families, until October 17, 1711.

At that time, the General Court issued this Reversal of Attainder:

"An Act to reverse the Attainders of George Burroughs and others for witchcraft.

"Forasmuch as in the year of our Lord one thousand six hundred ninety two, several towns, within this Province, were infested with a horrible witchcraft or possession of devils; and at a Special Court of Oyer and Terminer, held at Salem in the County of Essex, in the same year 1692. George Burroughs of Wells, John Proctor, George Jacobs, John Willard, Giles Corey and [Martha] his wife, Rebecca Nurse and Sarah Good, all of Salem aforesaid, Elizabeth How of Ipswich, Mary Easty, Sarah Wild and Abigail Hobbs all of Topsfield, Samuel Wardwell, Mary Parker, Martha Carrier, Abigail Faulkner, Ann Foster, Rebecca Eames, Mary Post, and Mary Lacy, all of Andover, Mary Bradbury, of Salisbury, and Dorcas Hoar of Beverly were severally indicted, convicted and attained of witchcraft and some of them put to death, others lying under the like sentence of the said Court, and liable to have the same executed upon them.

"The influence and energy of the evil spirits, so great at that time, acting in and upon those who were the principal accusers and witnesses, proceeding so far as to cause a prosecution to be had of persons of known and good reputation, which caused a great dissatisfaction and a stop put thereunto, until their Majesties' pleasure should be known therein. And upon a representation thereof, accordingly made by her late Majesty Queen Mary, the second, of blessed memory, by her royal letter, given at her Court at Whitehall, the fifteenth of April, 1693. Was graciously pleased to approve the care and circumspection therein; and to will and require that in all proceedings against persons accused of witchcraft, or being possessed by the Devil, the greatest moderation and all due circumspection be used, so far as the same may be without impediment to the ordinary course of justice.

"And some of the principal accusers and witnesses in those dark and severe prosecutions have since discovered themselves to be persons of profligate and vicious conversation.

"Upon the humble petition and suit of several of the said persons and of the children of others of them, whose parents were

143

executed. Be it declared and enacted by his Excellency the Governor, Council and Representatives in General Court, assembled and by the authority of the same; that the several convictions, Judgments and Attainders against the said George Burroughs, John Proctor, George Jacobs, John Willard, Giles Corey and [Martha] his wife, Rebecca Nurse, Sarah Good, Elizabeth How, Mary Easty, Sarah Wild, Abigail Hobbs, Samuel Wardwell, Mary Parker, Martha Carrier, Abigail Faulkner, Ann Foster, Rebecca Eames, Mary Post, Mary Lacy, Mary Bradbury and Dorcas Hoar, and every of them, be and hereby are reversed, made and declared to be null and void to all intents, constructions and purposes whatsoever, as if no convictions, Judgments or Attainders had ever been had, or given. And that no penalties or forfeitures of goods or chattels, be by said Judgments and Attainders, or either of them had, or incurred.

"Any law, usage or custom to the contrary not withstanding. And that no sheriff, constable, jailer or other officer, shall be liable to any prosecution in the law for anything they then legally did in the execution of their respective offices."

This reversal restored the civil rights and good names of all those whose relatives had petitioned the court. A letter had been sent to Judge Samuel Sewall by Nehemiah Jewett. It read as follows:

"Mister Sewall Sir; I thought good to return to you the names of several persons that were condemned and executed that no person or relative appeared in behalf of, for the taking of the Attainder, or for other expenses. They, I suppose, were returned to the General Court's consideration, to act upon according to their best prudence. Bridget Bishop alias Oliver, Susanna Martin, Alice Parker, Ann Pudeator, Wilmott Reed and Margaret Scott."

The sad significance of this was that these six people would remain convicted in the eyes of the law, since no one had appeared in their defense.

In 1957, the descendants of Ann Pudeator petitioned the Commonwealth of Massachusetts. The General Court passed a Resolve on August 28, saying that Ann Pudeator and others may have been prosecuted illegally, according to a shocking law of the period, for the crime of witchcraft, and that the descendants should be absolved from all guilt and shame - putting an end to the generations of misery caused by a few bored children.

CHAPTER XIV

APOLOGIES AND CONFESSIONS

The Jury wrote the following humble apology for their part in the trials.

"We whose names are underwritten, being in the year 1692 called to serve as jurors in the court of Salem, on trial of many who were by some suspected guilty of doing acts of witchcraft upon the bodies of sundry persons.

"We confess that we ourselves were not capable to understand, nor able to withstand, the mysterious delusions of the powers of darkness and Prince of the air, but were, for want of knowledge in ourselves and better information from others, prevailed with to take up with such evidence against the accused as, on further consideration and better information, we justly fear was insufficient for touching the lives of any (Deuteronomy 17:6), whereby we fear we have been instrumental, with others, though ignorantly and unwittingly, to bring upon ourselves and this people of the Lord, the guilt of innocent blood; which sin, the Lord saith in Scripture, he would not pardon (2 Kings 24:4); that is, we suppose, in regard of his temporal judgments.

"We do therefore hereby signify to all in general, and especially to the surviving sufferers, our deep sense of, and sorrow for, our errors in acting on such evidence to the condemning of any person; and do hereby declare that we justly fear that we were sadly deluded and mistaken, for which we are much disquieted and distressed in our minds, and do therefore humbly beg forgiveness, first, of God, for Christ's sake, for this our error, and pray that God would not impute the guilt of it to ourselves or others; and we also pray that we may be considered candidly and aright by the living sufferers, as being then under the power of a strong and general delusion, utterly unacquainted with, and not experienced in, matters of that nature.

"We do heartily ask forgiveness of you all, whom we have

justly offended; and do declare, according to our present minds, we would, none of us, do such things again, on such grounds, for the whole world; praying you to accept of this in way of satisfaction for our offense, and that you would bless the inheritance of the Lord that he may be entreated for the land.

"Thomas Fisk, Foreman, Thomas Pearly Senior, William Fisk, John Peabody, John Bacheler, Thomas Perkins, Thomas Fisk Junior, Samuel Sayer, John Dane, Andrew Elliot, Joseph Evelith, Henry Herrick Senior."

Samuel Sewall's diary contains the following entry concerning his address to the congregation on Fast Day, January 14, 1697. Fast Day was a day designated to atone for the wrongful deaths caused by the witch trials.

"Copy of the bill I put up on fast day; giving it to Mister Willard as he passed by, and standing up at the reading of it, and bowing when finished; in the afternoon.

"Samuel Sewall, sensible of the reiterated strokes of God upon himself and family; and being sensible that as to the guilt contracted, upon the opening of the late Commission of Oyer and Terminer at Salem (to which the order for this day relates) he is, upon many accounts, more concerned than any that he knows of, desires to take the blame and shame of it, asking pardon of men, and especially desiring prayers that God, who has an unlimited authority, would pardon that sin and all other his sins; personal and relative. And according to his infinite benignity, and sovereignty, not visit the sin of him, or of any other, upon himself or any of his, nor upon the land. But that he would powerfully defend him against all temptations to sin, for the future; and vouchsafe him the efficacious, saving conduct of his Word and Spirit."

What happened to the afflicted children after the witchcraft hysteria is for the most part unknown. Mary Walcott and Elizabeth Booth were married. From all accounts, Ann Putnam Junior lived a sad and lonely life. She was mostly an invalid. Her conscience wouldn't leave her alone, so, with the assistance of Reverend Green and the auspices of Samuel Nurse, she drew up a confession. Public announcements were made and a large throng of people gathered at the meetinghouse. Standing before the congregation as they sat in silence, she listened while the pastor read her confession from the church book:

"I desire to be humbled before God for that sad and humbling providence that befell my father's family in the year about ninety-two; that I, then being in my childhood, should, by such a providence of God, be made an instrument for the accusing of several persons of a grievous crime, whereby their lives were taken away from them, whom, now I have just grounds and good reason to believe they were innocent persons; and that it was a great delusion of Satan that deceived me in that sad time, whereby I justly fear I have been instrumental, with others, though ignorantly and unwittingly, to bring upon myself and this land the guilt of innocent blood; though, what was said or done by me against any person, I can truly and uprightly say, before God and man, I did it not out of any anger, malice, or ill will to any person, for I had no such thing against one of them; but what I did was ignorantly, being deluded by Satan.

"And particularly, as I was a chief instrument of accusing Goodwife Nurse and her two sisters, I desire to lie in the dust, and to be humble for it, in that I was a cause, with others, of so sad a calamity to them and their families; for which cause I desire to lie in the dust, and earnestly beg forgiveness of God, and from all those unto whom I have given just cause of sorrow and offense, whose relations were taken away or accused.

"Signed, Ann Putnam."

"This confession was read before the congregation, together with her relation, August 25, 1706, and she acknowledged it.

"Joseph Green, Pastor."

Stricken with continuously-recurring illness, Ann died in 1716 at the age of thirty-six.

BIBLIOGRAPHY

Boyer, Paul, and Stephen Nissenbaum, eds. *The Salem Witchcraft Papers: Verbatim Transcripts of the Legal Documents of the Salem Witchcraft Outbreak of 1692.* Three vols. New York: DaCapo Press, 1977.

Boyer, Paul, and Stephen Nissenbaum, eds. *Salem-Village Witchcraft: A Documentary Record of Local Conflict in Colonial New England.* Belmont, Calif.: Wadsworth Publishing Company, 1972.

Boyer, Paul, and Stephen Nissenbaum. *Salem Possessed: The Social Origins of Witchcraft.* Cambridge, Mass.: Harvard University Press, 1974.

Brown, David C. *A Guide to the Salem Witchcraft Hysteria of 1692.* Worcester, Mass.: Mercantile Printing Company, 1984: reprint ed. 1988.

Burr, George L., ed. *Narratives of the Witchcraft Cases: 1648-1706.* New York: Charles Scribner's Sons, 1914; reprint ed., New York: Barnes and Noble, 1975.

Hale, John. *A Modest Enquiry into the Nature of Witchcraft.* Boston: 1702; facsimile reproduction, Bainbridge, New York: York Mail-Print, 1973.

Hutchinson, Thomas. *The History of the Colony and Province of Massachusetts-Bay.* Three vols. Edited by L.S. Mayo. Cambridge, Mass.: Harvard University Press, 1936.

Nevins, Winfield S. *Witchcraft in Salem Village in 1692.* Boston: Lea and Shepard, 1892.

Richardson, Katherine W. *The Salem Witchcraft Trials.* Boston; The Book Department, Inc. 1983: reprint ed. 1988.

Thomas, M. Halsey, ed. *The Diary of Samuel Sewall, 1674-1729.* Two vols. New York: Farrar, Straus and Giroux, 1973.

Upham, Charles W. *Salem Witchcraft.* Two vols. Boston: Wiggins and Lunt, 1867; reprint ed., Williamstown, Mass.: Corner House Publishers, 1971.

Woodward, W. Elliot, *Records of Salem Witchcraft: Copied from the Original Documents.* Two vols. Privately Printed for W. Elliot Woodward, Roxbury, Mass., 1864/1865: reprint ed. New York: DaCapo Press, 1969.

152